INSIDE THE
GAS CHAMBERS

INSIDE THE GAS CHAMBERS

EIGHT MONTHS IN THE SONDERKOMMANDO OF AUSCHWITZ

SHLOMO VENEZIA

in collaboration with Béatrice Prasquier

Foreword by Simone Veil
Historical notes and additional material by
Marcello Pezzetti and Umberto Gentiloni
Edited by Jean Mouttapa
Translated by Andrew Brown

polity

Published in Association with the United States Holocaust Memorial Museum

First published in French as *Sonderkommando – Dans l'enfer des chambres à gaz*
© Éditions Albin Michel S.A.-Paris, 2007

This English edition © Polity Press, 2009
Reprinted 2011 (three times), 2012 (four times), 2013 (twice),
2014 (three times), 2015 (three times), 2016 (twice),
2017 (twice), 2018 (twice)

Polity Press
65 Bridge Street
Cambridge CB2 1UR, UK

Polity Press
350 Main Street
Malden, MA 02148, USA

ISBN-13: 978-0-7456-4383-0
ISBN-13: 978-0-7456-4384-7 (pb)

A catalogue record for this book is available from the British Library.

Typeset in 10.75 on 14 pt Adobe Janson by
Servis Filmsetting Ltd, Stockport, Cheshire
Printed and bound in Great Britain by Clays Ltd, Elcograf S.p.A.

The assertions, arguments and conclusions contained herein are those of the
author or other contributors. They do not necessarily reflect the opinions of
the United States Holocaust Memorial Museum.

Every effort has been made to trace all copyright holders, but if any have
been inadvertently overlooked the publishers will be pleased to include any
necessary credits in any subsequent reprint or edition.

For further information on Polity, visit our website: www.politybooks.com

I dedicate this book to my two families: my family from before the war, and my family from after it. My first thoughts go to my dearest mother – only forty-four years old at the time of these events – and my two young sisters, Marica and Marta, then fourteen and eleven, respectively. I often think sadly of the difficult life my mother had, being widowed very young with five children. Making many sacrifices, and struggling against almost insuperable difficulties, she brought us up in accordance with wholesome principles, such as being honest and respecting people. These sacrifices and these sufferings all counted for nothing, as they were wiped out at the same time as were my young sisters, no sooner than they had climbed out of the cattle cars onto the *Judenrampe* of Auschwitz-Birkenau on April 11, 1944.

My other family came into being after the great tragedy. My wife Marika and my three sons, Mario, Alessandro, and Alberto, know many things better than I do and base their lives on the essential principles of honesty and respect for others. My wife's tenacity has meant that they have managed to grow up into men I can be proud of. Marika has also taken great care of me, and lightened the burden of the infirmities that ensued from my imprisonment in the camps. She deserves more than my silent affection. Thank you, Marika, for all you have done up until now and all that you continue to do with our six grandchildren: Alessandra, Daniel, Michela, Gabriel, Nicole, and Rachel, and our daughters-in-law, Miriam, Angela, and Sabrina.

Your husband, father, and grandfather,
Shlomo Venezia

The whole truth is much more tragic and terrible.

Zalmen Lewental*

* Zalmen Lewental's manuscript in Yiddish was discovered in October
1962, buried in the yard of the Auschwitz Crematorium. It was written
shortly before the outbreak of the Sonderkommando revolt, so as to leave
an eye-witness account and some trace of the extermination of the Jews
in the gas chambers. Lewental seems to have died in November 1944,
only a few weeks before the Liberation. Taken from "Des voix sous la
cendre: Manuscrits des Sonderkommandos d'Auschwitz-Birkenau," ed.
by Georges Bensoussan, *Revue d'histoire de la Shoah*, no. 171 (January–
April 2001).

CONTENTS

FOREWORD

by Simone Veil

Shlomo Venezia arrived in Auschwitz-Birkenau on April 11, 1944; I arrived there myself, from Drancy, four days later. Until September 9, 1943, we had lived – he in Greece, I in Nice – under Italian occupation, with the feeling of being, at least provisionally, safe from deportation. But, after the capitulation of Italy, the Nazi vise immediately tightened, both on those who lived in the Alpes-Maritimes and on those in the Greek archipelago.

When I speak of the Shoah, I often refer to the deportation and extermination of the Jews of Greece, since what happened in that country illustrates perfectly the fierce tenacity with which the Nazis pursued the "Final Solution," hunting down the Jews even in the smallest and most remote islands of the archipelago. So it was with particular interest that I read the story of Shlomo Venezia, a Jew, an Italian citizen, who speaks not only Greek but also Ladino, the dialect of the Jews of Salonika where he lived. His name, Venezia, refers to the time when his ancestors, in the years of wandering that followed the expulsion of the Jews from Spain in 1492, had traveled to Italy before moving on to Salonika, the "Jerusalem of the Balkans," ninety percent of whose Jewish community was exterminated during the Second World War.

I have read many accounts written by former deportees, and each time they take me back to life in the camp. But the story told by Shlomo Venezia is especially overwhelming because it is the only complete eye-witness account that we have from a survivor of the Sonderkommandos. Now we know precisely how they were condemned to perform their abominable task, the worst task of all: that of helping the deportees who had been selected for death to get undressed and to enter the gas chambers, then of taking away all those corpses, bodies intertwined with each other in their death struggles, to the crematorium ovens. As they were unwilling accomplices of the executioners, almost all of the members of the Sonderkommando were murdered, just like those they had led to the gas chambers.

The force of this eye-witness account comes from the irreproachable honesty of its author. He relates only what he himself saw, leaving nothing out: neither the worst, such as the barbarity of the man in charge of the Crematorium, nor the summary executions or the uninterrupted functioning of the gas chambers and the crematorium ovens; he also speaks of what might attenuate the horror of the situation, such as the relative mercy shown by a Dutch SS officer, or the less atrocious conditions of survival that the members of the Sonderkommando received relative to those of the other deportees, since the Sonderkommandos were the indispensable servants of the machinery of death. Another thing that makes his account exceptional is that only when he engaged in this dialogue with Béatrice Prasquier did Shlomo Venezia dare to mention the most macabre aspects of his "work" in the Sonderkommando, adding details of unbearable horror that bring out the full extent of this abominable Nazi crime.

With his simple words, Shlomo Venezia gives new life to the emaciated faces, with their exhausted, resigned, and often terror-stricken eyes, of those men, women, and children whom he is seeing for the last time. There are those who are unaware of the fate that awaits them; those who, coming from the ghettos, fear that there is little hope of surviving; and finally those who, being selected in the camp, know that death awaits them – but then, for many of the latter, death comes as a deliverance.

A glimmer of humanity sometimes lightens the horror in which Shlomo Venezia tries to survive in spite of everything. There is his meeting, at the threshold of the gas chamber, with his uncle Léon Venezia, who is now too weak to work, and Shlomo's attempt to give him a final bite to eat. The younger man can lavish one last gesture of tenderness on the older and then recite a *kaddish* in his memory. There's also the harmonica Shlomo sometimes plays. And finally, there are those gestures of solidarity which help him remain a human being.

Shlomo Venezia does not try to hide the episodes that might give rise to criticism, should anyone dare to formulate it. It redounds entirely to his honor that he is brave enough to speak of his feeling of complicity with the Nazis, of the selfishness he sometimes needed to survive, but also of his desire for vengeance at the liberation of the camps. There are those who might suggest that, having been in a kommando where he was given better food and better clothes, he perhaps suffered less than the other deportees. Shlomo Venezia asks such people: what is a bit more bread worth, or extra rest, or a few more clothes, when every day your hands are steeped in death? Because he also experienced the "normal" conditions of life in the camps which he describes with exceptional precision and truthfulness, Shlomo Venezia unhesitatingly declares that he would rather have died a slow death than have had to work in the Crematorium.

So how to survive in that hell, when the only thing to which one can look forward is the moment when one is going to be killed oneself? To this question, every deportee has his or her own answer. For many people, such as Shlomo Venezia, one had to stop thinking. As he says: "During the first two or three weeks, I was constantly stunned by the enormity of the crime, but then you stop thinking." Every day he would have preferred to die, and yet each day he struggled to survive.

That Shlomo Venezia is still here today represents a double victory over the process of extermination of the Jews; for, in each of the members of the Sonderkommando, the Nazis wanted to kill the *Jew* and the *eye-witness*, to commit the crime and eradicate all trace of it. But Shlomo Venezia has survived and has told his story, after a long period of silence, like many other former deportees. If he, as did I and many others, spoke only belatedly, it is because nobody wished to listen to us. We had returned from a world where they had tried to banish us from the human race; we wanted to say as much, but we encountered incredulity, indifference, and even hostility from others. It was only in the years after the deportation that we found the courage to speak because, in the end, people did listen to us.

That is why this account, like those of all deportees, needs to be understood by each person as an appeal to reflection and vigilance. Over and above what he teaches us about the Sonderkommandos, Shlomo Venezia reminds us of that absolute horror, that "crime against humanity": the Shoah. Shlomo Venezia's voice, like that of all the deportees, will fall silent one day, but this dialogue between him and Béatrice Prasquier will remain, a dialogue between a witness who saw everything, one of the last to do so, and a young woman, a representative of the new generation, who was able to listen to him because she herself has for years been devoting a large part of her life to the struggle against forgetting. She deserves our thanks, particularly for having the courage to accompany Shlomo Venezia in his overwhelming return to the past.

It is now the task of this younger generation not to forget, and to ensure that Shlomo Venezia's voice will be heard forever.

Simone Veil
President of the Fondation pour la Mémoire de la Shoah

NOTE

by Béatrice Prasquier

This account was compiled from a series of interviews I had with Shlomo Venezia in Rome, with the help of the historian Marcello Pezzetti, between April 13 and May 21, 2006. The conversations were conducted in Italian and then translated and transcribed as faithfully to the original as possible and revised by Shlomo Venezia so as not to diminish the authenticity of his story.

Since he was at the heart of that machine designed to pulverize human lives, Shlomo Venezia is one of the few survivors able to bear witness to the "absolute" victims, those drowned amid the multitude of forgotten faces not saved by chance and an exceptional fate.

His witness goes beyond an act of memory; it is a historical document that sheds light on the darkest moment in our history.

ACKNOWLEDGMENTS

I am very grateful to the American Jewish Joint Distribution Committee for all that they did for me and for many survivors throughout Europe. It's thanks to them that I am still alive today.

I must also thank the Prasquier family, from Paris, of whom I am very fond. Thanks to all the people who were with me and gave me the moral support that enabled me to get through the terrible moments of the Second World War.

Finally, I would like to thank all the historians, researchers, teachers, and pupils whom I have had occasion to meet during my various appearances in their institutes or during visits to Auschwitz, especially those who, in one way or another, have contributed to this book: Marcello Pezzetti, Umberto Gentiloni, Béatrice Prasquier, Maddalena Carli, and Sara Berger.

S.V.

1

LIFE IN GREECE BEFORE THE
DEPORTATION

My name is Shlomo Venezia, and I was born in Salonika, Greece, on December 29, 1923. My family had been forced to leave Spain when the Jews were expelled in 1492, but before settling in Greece, they spent time in Italy. That's why my name is Venezia. The Jews who came from Spain did not, at that time, have family names; they were called (for example) Isaac son of Solomon. On arriving in Italy, they chose for themselves family names corresponding to the name of the city to which they had moved, in this instance Venice. That's why many Jewish families bear the names of cities. In our case, this was what enabled us to keep Italian citizenship.

There were five children in our family, two boys and three girls. My older brother, Maurice, was two and a half years older than I; next came Rachel, who was one year and two months older than I. Then the last two daughters, Marica, born in 1930, and, after her, Marta, born in 1933. For the first years, my family lived in a house. It wasn't very big, but it was better than the wooden shacks in which most of the poorer Jews of Salonika lived. As the family grew, the house became too small. I must have been five when we sold it and built a bigger, two-story house next door, on a piece of land belonging to my grandfather. My father was a bit egocentric, and he had his name written in red bricks on the path leading to the front door. The upper floor was rented out to Greek families. The money from their rent helped my father to pay his taxes. Unfortunately, things changed with his death, which happened very early. It must have been 1934 or 1935, and he left five fatherless children behind.

So you were very young. How did you react to his death?

I was eleven, I was at school when one of my father's female cousins came to take me to see him in the hospital. He'd had an operation for a kidney problem, but nothing further could be done. In any case, I didn't even have time to see him; he died before I arrived. All at once, we found ourselves almost alone, without material support. My father had run a small barbershop that his father had built for him. I obviously couldn't step into his shoes on his death, since I was still too young. So his assistant took it over in exchange for a small percentage that he paid my family every week. But it wasn't enough to feed a family of five children. It was only thanks to the help of my mother's four brothers that we managed to have enough to eat every day. I went to their place every Thursday to pick up a bag of vegetables – eggplants, onions, and other things that they grew and put aside for their sister. This help was indispensable but not enough; as a result, one year after my father's death I had to leave school to find a job and to help support my family financially. I was barely twelve years old.

And what did your older brother do?

He was sent by the Italian consulate to study in Milan. My father had fought in the First World War, and he was an Italian citizen, so he'd had the right to certain privileges. And that also meant we had one fewer mouth to feed. When the racial laws were passed in Italy in 1938, my brother was excluded from the Marchioni Technical Institute in Milan and sent back to Greece. So he never finished his studies either.

My father never lived to see the years in which the Fascist regime showed its true face. He felt so proud to be an Italian in Greece that he didn't hesitate to wear the black shirt of the new regime and to march proudly along in the processions whenever the occasion presented itself. In his view, Mussolini was a socialist, and he never understood the real nature of Fascism. We were too distant to see which way this regime was drifting. As an ex-soldier, he took part in all the demonstrations and parades organized by the Italians. It was his only break from everyday life. It gave him a feeling of prestige vis-à-vis the other Jews of Salonika. Not very many of the Jews who'd come from Italy had kept their Italian nationality. Most of them adopted the same attitude as my father: they saw the realities from a distance, without really understanding what was happening in the Italian cities.

Did you sense any difference in Salonika between Italian Jews and Greek Jews?

Of the sixty thousand Jews in the city, there must have been not many more than three hundred of us Jews of Italian origin. But we were the only ones who were authorized to send our children to the Italian school. In comparison with the others, who in general went to the Jewish school, this gave us certain advantages: we got everything free, we didn't have to pay for our books, we could eat in the canteen, we were given cod liver oil. . . . We wore really smart uniforms, with airplanes for the boys and swallows for the girls.

During this period, the Fascists were trying to promote Italian prosperity over all else. This was propaganda meant for the eyes of other countries, but we reaped the benefits. So, on Saturdays at school, there was the "Fascist Saturday," which all the pupils were supposed to attend. I felt proud to join in these processions; I felt different from the others, and I enjoyed this feeling. I even went twice to a holiday camp in Italy, with the Balilla,[1] whereas at that time hardly anyone ever traveled. And then we had several other advantages, since the Italian Embassy gave us a great deal of help. For example, on certain holidays, the consulate would hand out shoes and books to Italians who weren't so well off. For us, these things made quite a difference. Actually, the Jewish community in Salonika was divided into three categories: a tiny number were very rich, a marginal group managed to scrape by, but the vast majority of people would head off to work each morning not knowing whether they'd manage to bring back enough money to feed their families in the evening. It's difficult to admit, but at home I couldn't just say "I'm hungry, I'm going to have something to eat," since we had nothing. It was completely different from these days when you need to force children to finish up what's on their plates. Back then, everything was in short supply, and everyone had to do whatever they could to find something to eat. I remember that we had some neighbors who were even poorer than us. My mother always tried to help them, even though we were going short ourselves. This gives you an idea of the extreme poverty in which we found ourselves. All of this forged my character. I'm convinced that,

[1] Fascist youth movement.

when you have to go without all the time, it makes you a stronger person.

What was Jewish life in Salonika like?

There must have been five or six Jewish districts in the city, all very poor. They were generally designated by the number of the tramline that went there. But the main one was called Baron Hirsch, after a rich donor who'd helped the Jewish community of Salonika. Over ninety percent of the population who lived in this district were Jewish. Actually, we lived just outside this part of town, but I spent pretty much all my time with Jews. At home, everything was kosher. Not because my family was religious or really strict, but because all the shops in the area were kosher. Meat in particular, which we bought on the few occasions when we could afford it. We ate it on Fridays, with beans; that was how the poor feasted. If you wanted to eat non-kosher, you really had to be determined and look for it a long way outside your district. On the other hand, the food at school wasn't kosher, but this wasn't a problem as far as I was concerned. The main thing for us was just to eat so we wouldn't starve to death.

A lot of the Jews we lived amongst were religious. But probably not like in the little villages of Poland, where everyone really was very strict. When I had my bar mitzvah ceremony, I couldn't read Hebrew, so I learned my portion by heart. My father had already passed away, so it was my grandfather who took me to the synagogue. From then on, every time I went to sleep over at his house, he would wake me up at the crack of dawn to go and recite the morning prayer with him. Like all thirteen-year-old boys, who prefer to stay in bed, I'd roll over, grumbling, trying to get out of prayers.

What were the relations between Jews and non-Jews?

There weren't any particular problems. Even if most of my friends were Jewish, I also hung around with Christians. There could be the occasional scrap, though, when certain youths from other neighborhoods came into the Jewish district to provoke us and pick a fight with the Jews. But these were mainly just tussles between kids. I don't know if the word "anti-Semitism" was relevant here. I remember one episode that almost turned out really badly for me; I must have been twelve or thirteen. In those days we'd often go out on a Saturday evening to take a look at the girls from the other districts and maybe meet them. But the boys soon started to get jealous and tried to send us packing – it was their territory. Once, I found myself with four or five friends confronting a gang from another part of town. My friends turned and fled, but I was unaware of the danger and continued walking. When I saw how angry they were, I started to pretend I had a limp. As they went by they said, "We'll let you off since you've got a limp – otherwise . . . .." I limped along for another dozen steps or so, and then took to my heels. These are things that all children do.

But you didn't sense there was any particular hostility towards the Jews . . .

The only time when you felt an unpleasant tension was the Orthodox Easter. In the cinemas, you could see short films that fueled anti-Semitism, saying that the Jews killed Christian children and used their blood to make unleavened bread. Those were the most difficult times, but I don't remember it turning violent. On the other hand, you did feel that being Jewish wasn't easy when there was a change of government and a Fascist government came to power. Then Jews had a lot more problems. Even when it was the other boys who

came spoiling for a fight, the Jews were always held responsible. But in other ways we were so out of it all that few of us
knew what was happening in Germany all this time. Anyway,
right up until the end, nobody ever could have imagined it.
You know, we didn't have a telephone, and no radio except in
the two town taxis. One of the two drivers was Jewish and
when we went past his car we could hear someone talking in a
strange voice; it was the radio. We were intrigued by this, and
wanted to know how this radio thing worked. But in any case,
I was too young to take any interest in what it was saying.

*So at the age of twelve you had to look after yourself and leave school
to get a job . . .*

Yes, I didn't have any external support to encourage me and
help me with my studies. My mother had been born in Greece
but didn't even speak Greek; that was because her parents, like
a lot of Jews, didn't want their daughters to socialize with non-
Jews. The language I spoke at home was always Ladino, the
Judeo-Spanish dialect. But with my friends, out in the streets,
I always spoke Greek. I spoke it perfectly, without the accent
and intonations that were particular to the Jews of Salonika.
All I knew I had picked up in the streets. I hadn't been to the
Jewish school, and hardly to the Italian one either. My father
was no longer around to teach me about life and my mother
merely gave me a bit of practical advice. In poor families, the
main worry wasn't education but just getting enough to eat.
We just grew, out in the open air.

So at twelve I started to do small jobs. I'd do anything I
could find, just to take a bit of money home and help my
mother. For instance, for a few months I worked in a little factory that made mirrors. I was still just a lad, but they put me
on the press; I had to attach the mirror to the handle. Then I
worked in the factory of one of my father's friends, an Italian

– he wasn't Jewish. He produced thermosiphons. Right near where we lived I also worked in a factory that made beds. I did odd jobs, carrying this, fetching that . . . it wasn't much, but it made all the difference to my mother.

My brother was still in Italy and neither my mother nor my sisters worked. My mother had married while still very young and had gotten nothing out of life apart from us, her children. She devoted herself entirely to her family and did all she could for us. I remember that her only relaxation, when we were still little, was going out on Sunday evenings. My parents would take us to a little place that sold various kinds of beer and cheese. They'd sit down at a table and order a beer or two and the waiter would bring a little cheese. We never left them alone, we were always asking for a little bit. In the end, my mother had none left for herself. I have kept these memories, even if they make me sad. I've often thought about what I could have done to help my mother. I loved her so much and I know that she was especially fond of me. Her name was Doudoun Angel Venezia. I know all the sacrifices she made for us, I made an effort to help her as much as I could, but I'd like to have done more.

But I was still young and I, too, wanted to enjoy life. For instance, I tried to put a few coins aside so I could rent a bicycle for a little while. I loved doing that. After all, I got by on my own. Since I couldn't buy a bike, I managed to build myself a kid's scooter. I used a long piece of wood, with another one as the handlebars, two wheels that I'd found – and I racked my brains to invent some way of getting the handlebars to turn. I managed it, but before I could go scooting, I had to walk two or three hundred yards to find a road I could use. This scooter was the occasion of my first big disappointment as a child. The first day I went out to give it a try, I was proud and very happy. I slung it across my shoulders, and walked past a cart that had come to a stop. The road was really muddy and the horse couldn't pull the cart. When he saw me coming by, the man driving the cart took my scooter without so much as a by-your-leave, and used it to thwack the horse, which took fright and heaved itself out of the mud that was holding it back. My scooter lay on the ground, completely broken. All I could do was start to cry. He took my scooter, broke it, the horse got out of the mud – and I was stuck in it. You can imagine how disappointed a youngster must have been when he'd put all his energies into putting this toy together. It was one of life's lessons.

Did things change when your brother came back from Italy?

He came back in 1938, after the promulgation of the laws excluding the Jews from school in Italy. The situation at home didn't change much. I was a bit cross with him – instead of thinking about the family, he was thinking only of himself, going off to have fun. . . . I think he resented my mother for having sent him so far away. He and I weren't all that close: he had his gang, and I had mine. Even though my sister was older than I, I played the role of the big protective brother with her. I even remember that, one day, I tore a blouse that she'd sewn herself – I thought it was too low-cut. . . .

The war was brewing. How did the people around you react, and how did the start of hostilities affect you?

We didn't really realize what was happening. The community leaders got together to discuss it. They were worried, and they searched in the Torah to try to interpret events. But it was all so far away from us. We'd heard certain things about Germany. All we knew was that the German regime had it in for Jews. We were so hungry and had so many problems with our own lives that we didn't have time to wonder about the future. This is why, later on, the Germans had no difficulty at all in deporting the Jews from Greece. The Germans easily persuaded them that the occupation forces were going to allocate lodgings to them depending on the size of each family – the men would go off to work and the women would stay at home. We were naïve and didn't know what was happening politically. And then, I suppose that people thought the Germans were precise, decent people. When you bought something "made in Germany" it worked properly. It was precision-made. People believed what they were promised. They didn't have enough to eat, and here people were offering them a place to live in exchange for their labor – it didn't seem such a big deal. . . .

For us, the war really started with the invasion of Albania by Italy.[2] Even before entering Greece, Italy bombed the city of Salonika. The bombs set fire to the houses and terrified the populace. When Italy declared war, the Greek police immediately came to arrest all men of Italian nationality. I wasn't of age yet, so they left me, but they took my brother Maurice. A policeman I knew told me I could stay for the time being, but I'd need to make sure I didn't have anything in my pockets that might cause problems. I didn't immediately realize what he meant, but the fact was, if someone was found with a mirror in his pocket, he might be accused of having been signaling to the planes.

So they took my brother, but only him. They also took all the Italians, Jews and non-Jews, and put them into a big block in the city center. It wasn't a prison, but they weren't allowed out. The problem was that it was precisely this zone that the Italians bombed. Luckily, they weren't killed. They were then transferred to near Athens, and they weren't liberated until the Italians arrived. My cousin Dario Gabbai, who was there

---

[2] For more details, see the historical note on the situation in Greece and Italy during the war: pp. 189–96.

with them, with his brother and his father, told me that a Jew who was quite well-off had paid for the Italian Jews to be kept in a hotel under guard. At least they got to eat better there than at home.

All this time, I used to climb every day up onto the roof of a house occupied by soldiers of the Greek army. I knew that a truck came every day at the same time to hand out food to the soldiers. I'd made friends with them and, as they didn't suspect that I was of Italian nationality, they gave me some food as well. I had nothing to do, but at least I could eat. Things remained like this for three months: the Italians advanced, and were then driven back by the Greek army, they invaded and were then pushed back. Eventually, the Germans entered Greece from the north to help their Italian allies. This was bad news for us. Salonika, the main city in the north of Greece, was immediately occupied by the Germans. If the Italians had bombed the bridges and strategic sites instead of bombing the cities, it would have been easy for them to win – Greece didn't have much of an army. But instead of that, it was the Germans who overran Greece without encountering the slightest difficulty.

The day the German troops entered Salonika we were in a shelter situated under some big buildings, near the port and the warehouse. The house was right next to the railway station and the area was likely to be bombed, so we moved over to where my uncles lived. As usual, I was always on the lookout for something to eat. I saw there were people coming back from the port carrying supplies. They were helping themselves so as to leave nothing for the Germans. So I went down there and took a barrel of oil that I rolled back to where my family had taken shelter. On my way there, a restaurant owner came up and asked me if I was selling. I thought I could easily sell it and go back and get another one pretty quickly. We haggled a bit and he immediately gave me a nice bunch of banknotes. I left the oil with him and went back to the port, but there was nothing left. I returned to my mother and told her what had happened. "What have you gone and done?" she shouted. "We could have done something with that oil, but the money's no use at all." I went back to the restaurant owner with her. She begged him, and he finally agreed to give back half the oil I'd sold him.

On another occasion, I was luckier. I found a pancake-griddle and I managed to come away with a few of the cakes, since I knew my way round the warehouse. Everybody wanted to buy them from me, so I started to sell them, then I went back to the place I'd found them. In the meantime, people had closed it all up, but I spotted a little hole through which I managed to slip. I took everything I could get my hands on, and went back home with the pancakes and the money.

Once the Germans arrived, things got worse, and it was more and more difficult to find things to eat. As we were Italians, we received more help than the other Jews. There weren't many Italian soldiers, since the city was occupied by the Germans, but I struck up a friendship with some of the Italian troops. This made it easier for me to find food. In addition to this, the Italian consulate continued to help us by handing out, once a week, canned food, pasta and parmesan. There were six of us at home and this meant a lot of stuff to bring back. I'd take a trolley and head to the place where the food was distributed. On the way back, instead of coming down the normal road that was in good repair, I opted to take a short cut, down a rougher but quicker track. Once I was stopped by a Greek policeman who said:

"Hey, you there! Where'd you get those things?"

"I was given them. I'm Italian. It's my right."

"I don't believe you. You're coming with me to the station."

"Why? I haven't stolen anything. I'm entitled to it! Let me go home, please!"

I realized that all he wanted was a share of the booty. So I told him to come with me, and in exchange I'd give him some parmesan. He accepted and escorted me home. This misadventure meant that I didn't bump into another policeman who'd inevitably have asked the same thing. I met this policeman every week, and the same scene happened each time. In any case, if I'd had to take the high road I'd have been stopped by others. At least he protected me.

But since these supplies weren't enough, I started to barter, swapping things on the black market. Generally speaking, I'd spend my day with the others, waiting at the station for the military trains passing through. The Italian and German soldiers would get off for a while at the Salonika station, and we'd buy or sell what we could – cigarettes, for instance, or malaria drugs that one could take to the countryside to exchange for potatoes or for flour to make bread. You had to take the train and travel quite some distance to find things to exchange. To avoid paying for a train ticket, I used to hang on to the back of one of the train coaches, even when the weather was cold. It was hard, but I was young and healthy.

Once, when we were all leaning against a wall, waiting, a Greek policeman arrived and carted all of us off to the police station. All of us were Jews. He made us come into his office, one by one, to question us. I was the last, and I soon realized that the policeman was forcing each boy to open his hand, which would be beaten with an iron baton until the flesh bled. When it was my turn to go into the office, I told him:

"You can't touch *me* – I'm Italian!"

"I couldn't care less whether you're Italian or not, open your hand!" he ordered.

But my brother, who hadn't been with me when I was arrested, had learned that I was at the station, and he'd told an Italian soldier, someone we knew well. This soldier stormed into the office, and grabbed the policeman by his collar, yelling:

"He's Italian – you'd better watch yourself if you touch a single hair on his head!"

So being Jewish was of less importance than having Italian nationality?

Yes, we were protected for as long as the Italians were in Greece. And however much I was a Jew, at that period, I was still, above all, Italian. And this protected me, even from the Germans, who immediately started to persecute the Jews. When they needed people to work for them, they'd seal off the district and capture anyone trying to escape. Then they'd carry out a selection and keep the Jews. Sometimes I was present. On the square they'd assemble about forty Jews between eighteen and forty-five years old. To humiliate them, they'd make them do what they ironically called "gymnastics." The local Greeks would stand and watch – it was fun for them to see the Jews forced to carry out these ridiculous movements. Often, after this humiliation, the men were sent off to do forced labor in sites infested by malaria. They'd work there for a month or two and come back, ill and thin, more dead than alive.

I happened to be in the area once when they were rounding up people. It was before the Baron Hirsch district was closed. I knew the back streets well enough to be able to escape. Even though I was Italian and theoretically protected, it was better not to fall into their hands.

And then, one day, after someone high up in the SS had been visiting Salonika, orders were given to close the Baron Hirsch district and put barbed wire all round it. The area was definitely sealed off towards the end of 1942, or early 1943. The first deportations started three months later.

I also remember that a German who was working in the office of the Gestapo tried to warn the Jews. He had made friends with some of the community leaders and passed information on to them. This German vanished overnight. I imagine he was denounced by counter-espionage agents. . . .

What was the situation in the ghetto?

We didn't use the word "ghetto," we just said "Baron Hirsch." But it was like a ghetto, with an exit gate opposite the railway station and an entrance gate, under constant surveillance, on the other side of the district. The area soon became a place of passage before deportations.

They rounded up and imprisoned the elderly. As I've said, I lived just outside the area and I was still protected by my Italian nationality. I didn't wear the yellow star that they'd imposed on the Jews before sealing the district. And on the document from the consulate, stating that I was an Italian citizen, the fact that I was Jewish wasn't mentioned. My first name was given as "Salomone" and not "Shlomo." So I was able to stay on the Greek side and help my friends who were forced to stay in the district. They had nothing to eat, so they'd arrange to meet me in an out-of-the-way spot and throw me money over the fence so I could go and buy the food they needed. But I did this only with the people I knew. This procedure lasted barely a week, since they were soon deported and replaced by other Jews whom I didn't know.

I had no opportunity to see my uncles or my cousins before they were deported. I didn't even find out when they left. My grandmother on my father's side, Doudoun Levi Venezia, who was sixty-three, was deported too, even though, like my father, she had Italian nationality. But she lived inside the district, and in spite of all our efforts and Maurice's attempts to get her out, it wasn't possible to save her. Baron Hirsch had become a transit camp; no sooner was everything ready for the next deportation than the trains were already being filled. But the suffering began there, in the district.

Within ten days, the people living in Baron Hirsch had been deported; then they widened the circle of round-ups, arresting Jews from other districts and putting them into Baron Hirsch to replace the ones who'd gone. People slept barely one or two nights there before being deported, very early in the morning. In recent years, I've read in the Auschwitz Museum that during these first ten days, over ten thousand people were deported from Greece to Auschwitz.[3]

Did the Greeks witness these round-ups?

No, as the deportations were organized very early in the morning. There still wasn't anybody out and about. The schedule was chosen deliberately so that everything would go off without too many witnesses, discreetly. Even I never saw a thing.

Once the Germans had finished deporting all the Greek Jews, they wanted to start on the Italian Jewish families. The Consul, Guelfo Zamboni, intervened yet again to help us. I know that, after the war, he was awarded Yad Vashem's "Righteous Among the Nations" medal for saving many Jews, not only Italian Jews;[4] he also procured fake papers for Greek Jews so that they would be protected in the same way as the Italians. This time, he summoned the leaders of the Italian Jewish families. Instead of my father, my brother went to see

---

[3] Between March 1943 and August 1944, twenty-two convoys were deported from Greece to Auschwitz (over fifty-five thousand people), including nineteen convoys from Salonika, two from Athens and one from Rhodes. A convoy of Jews from Salonika also arrived in the Treblinka extermination camp in spring 1943.

[4] Guelfo Zamboni thus saved nearly two hundred and eighty people by giving them fake documents. Yad Vashem, in Israel, awarded him the "Righteous Among the Nations" title and medal in 1992.

him. The Consul told them that the Germans intended to deport us, but Italy was not going to let them. He gave us a choice between being transferred to Athens, which was still under Italian administration, or of being sent by boat to Sicily. Since some of the Italian Jews there had businesses, offices or factories in Greece, they preferred to stay in the vicinity to keep an eye on those enterprises. So they decided, in the name of all of us, to go to Athens. Unfortunately, this choice meant death, for virtually all of us.

How was the transfer to Athens organized?

It was in July. We left the house, carrying mattresses and everything that my sister had prepared for her wedding. Her fiancé wasn't Italian, and so he'd been deported in 1943 with his whole family.

The Italians had arranged for us to leave for Athens by train, under the protection of Italian soldiers who had been ordered not to let the Germans on board. Apparently, this transport was the cause of conflict between the two allies, but the Italians considered it an Italian matter. It took us two days to arrive, since the Germans tried in various ways to slow down our journey from Salonika to Athens. They used various stratagems, such as forcing the train to keep stopping so as to let more important convoys pass first, or leaving us for hours at a time on sidings. There were already tensions between the Germans and Italians. The Germans thought they could control everything, especially when it came to the Jews. The Italian soldiers gave my brother a weapon so that he could defend us if there was a problem. On our route, the train crossed zones infested with malaria, where the last Jews who had been rounded up for forced labor were working. The train driver, with the agreement of the Italian soldiers, slowed down to enable some of them to cling to the train and escape with us. One young boy climbed into our coach this way, and stayed in Athens under Italian protection.

When we finally reached Athens, they put us up in a school. People who had the means to rent an apartment did so. We were about twenty families staying in this school. The problem of food soon reappeared. Since we weren't working, we had to find some means of finding something to eat. The Italian Consulate gave us only one meal a day, and their aid obviously stopped on September 8, 1943, with the ending of their alliance with Germany.

Since there wasn't a black market in Athens, we had to find some other way. The elderly people with us in the school couldn't sell their things themselves, so they handed them over to me so that I could go and sell them at the flea market. In general, they had very fine traditional clothes, sewn with gold thread, and worn on festive occasions and holidays. They were very expensive outfits, but they had to be sold, even if they fetched just a few coins. Everyone needed food so badly. . . . I took what these people gave me, they told me how much they hoped to get for them, we came to an agreement, and if I managed to get a higher price for them, I kept the difference to feed my family. I very quickly understood that, when it came to selling these sorts of clothes, the best thing was to go to the brothels. They were rolling in money, since the women were never short of work. And they weren't concerned about how much the clothes cost, so long as they liked them; if you said "twenty," they paid twenty, without any argument. But for other things, you had to go to the market. It was there that I sold most of the objects that my sister had prepared for her dowry.

What happened after September 8, 1943?

The rumor immediately started going around that Italy had asked for an armistice. In Athens, as far as I knew, there were several thousand Italian soldiers, in the barracks and else-where. I'd had a chance to get to know quite a few of them. But the Germans completely took over and several soldiers refused to return to their barracks to sleep, in case they were taken prisoner by the Germans. At that time, I already was in contact with members of the Greek Resistance and I knew several families in the city. So I tried to place soldiers with families so that they wouldn't have to return to the barracks. I helped seven or eight in this way. I later learned that one of them had even married the daughter of the family in which I'd helped him to hide. In the meantime, I, too, tried to find shelter for my family. Since we had lost the protection of the Italians, there was no doubt that we in turn were going to be deported sooner or later.

The Germans started by sorting out the problem of the Italian soldiers. They told them that, if they wanted to continue the war on the side of the German forces, they'd have to register at an office. If, on the other hand, they wanted to go home, they'd have to present themselves at another office. The majority of them refused to continue fighting on the German side and so they did indeed go to register at the other office indicated. After a few days, they were informed that, to go home, they had to turn up at such-and-such a place at a particular time. This was a trap; they were loaded into train boxcars almost the same as those used to deport the Jews. I found out subsequently that they had been sent to do forced labor in German factories.

What did you do, in those circumstances, to make contact with the Resistance?

My brother and I had ended up getting to know and socialize with quite a few people in the district. When we realized that things weren't going to turn out well for us and that we'd soon be deported, we thought of joining the Resistance. We wanted to get our mother and sisters into the mountains, where they'd be safe. The problem was the Greek resistance fighters knew that we were Italian and they didn't really trust us. They told us they didn't need anyone else to join the Resistance out in the countryside, and if we wanted to be useful, we needed to stay in the city so as to help organize sabotage and pass on secret information.

So we started to carry out small acts of sabotage. This generally took place in the evenings, since we couldn't do anything in the daytime. There were too many people who might denounce us, too many spies, too many Greek soldiers collaborating with the Germans. So we'd go about it at night-time, in small groups. We'd split up, and each group took a district. We slipped leaflets under the doors, saying we'd come back the following day, and asking people to give us something, anything that would help. In general, people did help us, even if it was dangerous for them too. That's how we became *andartis*.[5]

Eventually, the resistance fighters found a place in the mountains where they could hide my mother and my sisters. My brother and I were to stay in town with a family. But the woman who was supposed to hide us was denounced before we arrived. My mother hid out for a while with my sisters in the village, but since she didn't speak Greek, she preferred to return to the school so as to be near us.

Didn't the Germans try to round up the Jews immediately after their entry into Athens?

No, in the first months, we didn't sense anything particular was going on. We had heard about Germany's military defeats

---

[5] Greek for "resistance fighter." The Greek Resistance Movement was called the Ethniko Apeleutherotiko Metopo or EAM (National Liberation Front).

and people were convinced that, in a situation where the Germans had other urgent things to attend to, they wouldn't bother to deport the Jews from Athens. In January or February 1944, they forced all the Jewish men to come and sign a register every Friday, in an office of the synagogue. I used to go with my brother, carrying a little suitcase, ready to flee at the slightest alert. But one Friday, it was around the end of March 1944, we made the mistake of going there early in the morning. On that particular day, instead of allowing us to leave, they made us go into the big synagogue hall, and the men who ran the synagogue asked us to remain there, with the other people who had come to sign. In theory we were supposed to be waiting for a German officer who was on his way. In fact, this was a pretext, made up by the Germans to get us in without any fuss. All the people who came along to sign were told to go into the synagogue. Around midday, on seeing that other people were still turning up, we realized that we'd been caught in a trap. The windows were very high and, to see what was happening outside, I climbed onto the shoulders of other boys. Outside, I could see several SS trucks and German soldiers carrying sub-machine guns and accompanied by dogs. I warned everyone that we were encircled and that if we didn't find a way of getting out of there as fast as possible they'd take us away. Most of the people there were Jews from Athens and the surrounding area. Unlike us Jews from Salonika, they hadn't witnessed any deportations and didn't know what the Germans were capable of. So they preferred to do nothing, certain that they would be killed if they tried to get out before the officer arrived. At around two in the afternoon the officer still hadn't come. But outside, everything was all ready. They ordered us to go out. We found ourselves facing trucks and armed soldiers encircling us. They yelled at us, "*Los! Los!*" "Move it! Move it!" and we had to climb into the trucks. I don't remember if there were any people standing around watching, but there must have been a few, even though they couldn't have managed to get very close.

The trucks took us to the big prison at Haidari. There must have been nearly a hundred and fifty of us. There wasn't any room for us in the main building. They dumped us into the shower block in the prison yard. There was nothing, no beds, no straw mattresses, just cement on the floor and showers over our heads. We were packed in tightly, and there was hardly any room to stretch out. It was really uncomfortable and difficult. In the yard we could hear regular shots – the summary executions of political prisoners. Our block was near the barbed wire and we were guarded by soldiers wearing a uniform that I didn't recognize, but resembling an Italian uniform. Stupid as I was, I spoke to one of the soldiers standing guard and told him, "I'm Italian! Do you think I could get away?" Of course, he immediately pointed his rifle at me, so I backed off and put my hands up, saying "Okay, drop it! I didn't say anything!" He was one of the Italian Fascists from the militia who collaborated with the Germans. In one sense, he saved my life, because if he had told me that I could try to escape, I certainly would have been killed; there were German soldiers at every corner, posted on watchtowers every twenty yards.

Did you really think you might have been able to escape?

Yes, all the time, since I knew what had happened in Salonika. If, in the synagogue, they'd listened to us when we tried to explain to them what the Germans had done in Salonika – the forced labor, the ghetto, and the deportations – perhaps they might have been able to force their way out, instead of waiting until it was too late. They could have escaped; they should have made the attempt. Some of them would surely have been killed but, in any case, they were heading to their deaths.

People kept on hoping that, if they did what they were told, they'd be spared. The reality was the complete opposite.

Who was there with you?

My brother and my cousins, Dario and Yakob Gabbai. Yakob was married, he was twelve years older than his brother Dario, who must have been twenty-one or twenty-two.

In addition to the little suitcase, I had on me five gold coins that my mother had entrusted to me. She'd also given five to my brother, but Maurice had immediately spent the money. My mother had taken those ten coins from among the jewels that her brothers and her parents had given to her before being deported. She had always categorically refused to take anything at all out of that envelope, since she was convinced that her brothers would return and would need that money to start up their lives again. Other people could have used this money to escape, but my mother was too honest and kept telling us: "Anyone who touches this money had better watch out!" Seeing that the situation was becoming serious, she had resigned herself to taking a few gold coins to give them to us, if our lives should be in danger. But in Haidari I almost lost the five coins that I had carefully preserved. . . .

And indeed, the day after we arrived in the prison some Germans turned up and, yelling and lashing out, they made us go out into the yard to line up five by five. After they'd picked up anything of interest from the empty hall, they settled down there and made us go in, in groups of five, ordering us to take off all our clothes so they could search us, and steal everything they wanted. Those who didn't immediately hand over any valuable objects in their possession were severely beaten.

I always used to make sure I was among the last in situations like this, so as to have time to see what was happening. All of a sudden, when half the people had gone through, I heard cries of pain coming from inside. The Germans were beating up a boy who'd hidden a gold coin in his trousers.

As well as my gold coins, I had a Doxa watch that I'd bought second-hand from a German, in exchange for cigarettes. Under the brand name there was an inscription: "Shimshi." This was the name of a Salonika Jew from whom the German had stolen the watch. This was the first watch I'd ever owned and I didn't want the Germans to get their hands on it. So I put it on the ground and crushed it, so that I would at least have the satisfaction of not letting them have it.

As for the gold coins, I decided to give one to my brother, one to Dario and one to Yakob, and to keep two on myself. I put the first coin into my mouth and swallowed it. They did the same. Except that in my case, the second coin didn't go down and I almost choked. I didn't have any bread or water, but it was out of the question that I was going to just choke to death there. So I worked up as much saliva as I could, and eventually the coin went down. In front of us, some idiots were spreading the rumor that the Germans had an X-ray machine. My brother was panic-stricken. I told myself that in any case it was too late and there wasn't anything else we could do to make the coins come out immediately. So I told myself, *"whatever will be, will be."*

When it was our turn to go in, the Germans hardly searched us. They'd probably picked up enough things and were in a hurry to finish. When we got back to the shower block, our little suitcase had vanished, but we'd been able to keep the main things. The next day, each of us went to the toilet to lay what I called "the golden egg." My cousin Dario went first; nothing. His brother Yakob; nothing. My brother said he didn't want to look. The second day, Dario laid "the golden egg," and so did my cousin Yakob and I. My brother; still nothing. He came to see us four days later to tell us that he too finally had laid "the golden egg."

How long did you stay in that prison at Haidari?

Seven or eight days. To begin with, I was furious that I'd allowed myself to get caught without trying to escape. Then, little by little, we had to get used to it. My brother, my cousins and I kept thinking over what we could have done, what we should have done.

Among us there were many people who came from other regions of Greece, from little villages in which there weren't more than a dozen or so Jews. They'd been captured and sent to Athens, as were, later on, some of the Jews of Corfu and Rhodes. And, once Salonika had been emptied, all the Jews who had been arrested had to pass through Athens. It had become the transit station.

Do you remember on what day you were deported?

It was the end of March or even April 1. We were imprisoned on the day of the Greek national holiday, March 25, and we stayed in prison for a week. I know the train arrived in Auschwitz on April 11, and I think the journey lasted for eleven days, so it must have been April 1.[6]

That day, the Germans made us go out into the yard. It was full of people. They told us to try to find members of our own families and to stay in groups with our relatives so that, when we reached our destination, they'd be able to allocate a house to us, depending on the size of each family. After looking around for a while, I managed to find my mother and my three sisters. My cousins also found their parents, their young brother Samy, and Yakob's wife. The fact that we were all

[6] Shlomo Venezia was deported in the first convoy to leave Athens. It arrived at Auschwitz-Birkenau on April 11, 1944. According to information from the Auschwitz Museum, the convoy consisted of two thousand five hundred Jews, but other sources indicate a higher number.

together reassured us. We tried to convince ourselves that the Germans were telling the truth and that we'd be given that house. We'd have to work hard, of course, but at least we'd be able to stay together. That was the main thing.

Then my mother told me that on the day my brother and I had been locked up, the Germans had searched the school and taken all those in it. My little sister Marica had been entrusted to a non-Jewish lady who lived near the school; my sister did the housework in exchange for meals and a roof over her head. But, when Monica learned that the Germans were going to deport her family, she ran off to join my mother. I've often told myself that if she hadn't known what was happening she'd definitely have stayed with that family and might have been saved. But things didn't work out that way and, unfortunately, she was deported too.

It was cunning of the Germans to get us together in our families. When you're alone, the idea of escaping is more tempting. But how can you think of abandoning your parents or your children? And yet, a few people did manage to escape, almost by chance. On the path between the prison and the freight station the trucks carrying us followed along one after the other. A German guard was seated near the driver and kept an eye on the passengers in the truck ahead. One of these trucks broke down and so, of course, the one ahead of it didn't have anybody to keep an eye on the rear. Five or six young boys jumped off and escaped, but the Germans soon had everything under control again.

We finally arrived on the platforms. There were cattle cars waiting for us. The Germans pushed us brutally into the wagons. Inside there was nothing, just planks on the floor, a big empty can in the middle, and a smaller one with water. In a corner, I saw three crates of raisins and carrots. The space was very limited, and as soon as everyone had climbed aboard, we saw that it would be impossible to stretch out; at best we would need to stay seated throughout the journey. I immediately sat in a corner near the window.

Men were starting to turn up near the station to start work – this is why the Germans wanted to hurry, so as not to attract too much attention. Looking out the window, I saw an SS officer starting to get angry with some people who seemed to be from the Red Cross. I thought they were there because they wanted to free us. But they simply wanted to hand out some food for our journey. I believe they knew what our final destination was, since they wouldn't have taken any trouble if it had been just a short trip, even in these conditions. Eventually they came to an agreement, and the SS officer allowed the Red Cross trucks to follow the train until it stopped outside the city. Through the window, I could see the trucks following us at a distance. The train stopped out in the open country, so that the Red Cross personnel could distribute parcels of food and blankets.

What were the windows of the carriage like? Was there barbed wire on them?

There were four little windows. In my carriage, the windows didn't have any barbed wire, but I saw that others did. This was definitely the first convoy to leave Athens and not all the carriages had yet been "adapted." When we reached Vienna, barbed wire was installed on our carriage. We felt even more oppressed, stifled, and humiliated. Until then, I had put my head out the window for almost the entire journey to get some fresh air and to see what was happening. This is what allowed me, at the beginning, to pick up a larger number of parcels. The Red Cross people tried to give us as many as they could, and the important thing was to grab hold of them. I picked up the parcels and the blankets, and threw them back to my brother and cousin, who were making room in the carriage.

After a few minutes, the officer yelled, "*Fertig!*" "That's it!" and ordered the Red Cross people to leave. As soon as they had gone, the soldiers went around the carriages to find out how many parcels everyone had received. I saw the German asking someone in the carriage ahead of ours how many he'd gotten. The young man replied that he'd gotten eight, and the German then ordered him to hand over four. In any case, they wouldn't have come into the carriages to check, that would have taken too much time; one just needed to say something plausible in reply to them. So when the German stopped in front of me and asked how many I had, I, too, replied that I had eight. As I'd anticipated, he directed me to throw out four. In fact, I'd picked up thirty-eight parcels and several blankets. In every parcel there were wheat wafers, powdered milk, chocolate, cigarettes, and other useful things to keep us going throughout the journey. Of course, we shared with the other people in the carriage. At least that way we had enough to survive the eleven days that the train journey lasted.

How many of you were in the carriages?

There must have been between seventy and eighty people. Among those deported in the carriages I knew several people who had been taken from Salonika at the same time as my family.

From Athens the train was meant to go via Salonika, which was an important railway junction in the north. The train stopped near the station to replenish its coal and water. I went up to the skylight to see if there was anyone outside I might recognize. German soldiers were posted every ten yards along the train. As chance would have it, the railway man who was checking the track was a young fellow I did know. His name was Gyorgos Kaloudis; he was five or six years older than I and had been a neighbor of mine when we were children. His father had also worked on the railways and was a known communist. The older man had been arrested by the Germans as soon as they entered Salonika. Gyorgos had replaced his father on the railways. His work consisted of ensuring that the brakes didn't block the wheels, and adjusting them with a long hammer. When he saw me, he appeared very surprised and slipped over, pretending to be working on my carriage. Without being noticed by the Germans, he said, in Greek, "What's going on? You here too? Try to get the hell out of here; where they're taking you, they just kill everybody!" He also told me that we were going to Poland. I wasn't able to ask him anything else; the Germans were keeping an eye on us.

When the train began to move again, I immediately told my brother and my cousins what Gyorgos had just told me. It had taken us two days to get from Athens to Salonika and it would be another two days before we got out of Greek territory. Up until then, we'd foolishly believed that the Greek resistance fighters would attack the train out in the open country to free us and prevent the deportations from happening. They'd promised they would do so, at the time we were with them. But Gyorgos's words made me realize that there was no point in waiting and that we had to try to escape by ourselves. But that meant leaving our families behind. . . . While we were on Greek territory, escaping would have been less dangerous – we would have found it relatively easy to hide out with the peasants. They'd have seen us as resistance fighters, rather than as Jews, and helped us. Once we were on Yugoslav territory things would start to get more difficult. So we tried to escape that evening.

We were thin enough to get out through the window and slip along the outside of the moving train. It was a big risk, since the Germans were keeping guard in turrets built on top of some of the carriages. I'd noted that one carriage in every three was occupied by SS. But we were determined. My brother was going to jump first, then I would. We'd have moved forward to join our cousins, who were going to jump after us. My brother didn't have time to stick his leg out. Already, everybody in the carriage had woken up and started yelling and crying. They were sure we were going to get ourselves killed and that they'd be killed too, for letting us escape. Dario's father, Milton, kept saying over and over, "They know how many of us there are. When the train reaches its destination and they see you're not there, they'll kill us all." In fact, this didn't change the outcome: all of them died anyway. But who could have known that then? When we saw them crying, when we saw how terrified and distraught my mother and sisters were, we began to feel that it wasn't fair to leave them alone were we to try to save ourselves. Had the others in the car not realized what we planned to do, we'd possibly have managed to escape and save ourselves. In any case, we tried again once more, the next day. But Milton stayed awake and kept an eye on us to stop us trying to get away. We held back as before. Eventually, we left Greek territory. We crossed Yugoslavia, then Austria. In Vienna, with the barbed wire installed, we finally lost all hope of freedom.

Were you able to speak with your mother during the journey?

No, I couldn't even get close to her, there was no room to move. To preserve a little privacy, a blanket had been spread out to separate the men from the women. A second blanket was used to curtain off the can that was used as a toilet. We could hardly move. In any case, we didn't talk much. Everyone was absorbed in his or her own thoughts and was sunk in gloom. There was nothing we could say to each other, as we were all in the same situation. We were there, finished; that was all. The idea of escape, of having wasted what was perhaps our only chance. . . . Everyone knew that we had nothing good to hope for. But I think it's usual to try to hang on to a shred of hope. That's why I didn't tell my family what I'd heard my childhood friend tell me.

Deep down, did you believe Gyorgos, or did you believe the Germans who told you that they were sending you to the East to work?

Both. On the one side, I wanted to convince myself that Gyorgos was merely peddling rumors and that it was absurd for the Germans to go to so much effort just to kill us as soon as we arrived. Nobody could believe that, but history has shown that Gyorgos was right. At that time, the Germans had already started to build the ramp that was to take the train right inside the camp. This was April 1944, and they were no longer so worried about non-German railway workers seeing the inside of the camp. I suppose that's how Gyorgos heard about what was happening in Auschwitz.

Did the train make any other stops?

Yes, it had already made one stop while we were still on Greek territory, so that the can we used as a toilet could be emptied. Actually, after just two days, the can was already overflowing, but we'd had to wait for that stop before they'd allow us to empty it. And in any case, that was the only time. Soldiers stood at a distance of fifteen yards or so to ensure that nobody would try to escape. When the doors of the carriage opened, I climbed out with three other boys, carrying the can that was full of excrement. We wanted to empty it right by the train, but the soldier told us to go a bit farther. Getting out of the carriage where we'd been shut up for several days, breathing the fresh air and seeing the daylight in that big open space made us feel really strange. It made it even harder to get back into the carriage. The carriage door stayed open for a quarter of an hour, but this was far from enough to refresh the air. We had to go back to the stench, that overpowering mixture of rubbish, excrement, and sweaty bodies.

Then the train crossed Yugoslavia and Austria. Once, when the train stopped again to pick up coal, I saw a man in uniform walking past, not carrying any weapons. I didn't know whether he was an Austrian soldier or a railway worker. He waved me over and said, "*Komm raus!*" "Get out!" I didn't trust him, I didn't know if he wanted to help me or to turn me in. He'd have won a medal for stopping me while I was trying to escape. I didn't do anything and the train continued on its way.

Do you remember having seen any other people outside the train, as you went through the different villages?

Yes, from time to time. In Brno, the train stopped again. I remember the place, as I'd found the name of the town distinctly odd. We were begging the Germans to let us have a little water. Instead of that, a drunkard stopped in front of my carriage and motioned to us in a very explicit dumb show, telling us we were all going to be killed, hanged. He was completely drunk, but seeing him waving his hands around like that made me so angry that I spat in his face the minute he came up to our carriage. Eventually, a German soldier shoved him away. When I think back to it, I don't know if he was doing it to make fun of us or whether he was simply trying to warn us. . . . After Brno, we took another two days to reach the *Judenrampe* in Auschwitz-Birkenau.[7]

---

[7] The first arrival and selection ramp for the convoys of Jews deported between March 1942 and May 1944, before the construction of the big ramp leading inside the camp (*Bahnrampe*). The *Judenrampe* is on the road between the camp at Auschwitz I and Birkenau. See the historical note (pp. 174–5) for more information.

Were there any deaths in your carriage?

No, in my carriage, nobody died. But this was certainly not the case in all the carriages. It suited the Germans if people were already dead on arrival. Traveling in conditions like that, for eleven days. . . . In my carriage, we had enough to eat on the first days, thanks to the Red Cross parcels, but the reserves were running out and nobody knew when we were going to arrive. People were starting to get seriously worried and agitated. We, the youngest people there, tried to calm them so that a general panic wouldn't spread and make the last days in the train even more difficult.

2

THE FIRST MONTH IN
AUSCHWITZ-BIRKENAU

The train hadn't blown its whistle when the transport had stopped en route. So when I heard that peculiar whistle and felt the train suddenly braking I immediately realized that the convoy had finally reached its destination. The doors opened onto the *Judenrampe*, just opposite the potato sheds. My first feeling was a sense of relief. I didn't know how much longer it would have been possible to survive in this train, without anything left to eat, without any space, air, or toilet facilities.

As soon as the train stopped, the SS opened the doors of the carriage and started yelling, "*Alle runter! Alle runter!*" "Everyone out! Everyone out!" We saw men in uniform pointing their sub-machine guns, and Alsatians barking at us. Everyone was in a stupor, numb after the journey – and all of a sudden, fierce yells and a whole infernal din to throw us off our guard, and prevent us knowing what was going on. I happened to be near the door, so I was among the first to climb out. I wanted to stay near the door to help my mother get out. We had to jump for it, as the carriage was high and the terrain was sloping. My mother wasn't that old, but I knew the journey had worn her out and I wanted to help her. While I was waiting for her, a German came up behind and struck me two heavy blows on the back of my neck with his stick. He lashed out with such force I thought he'd split my skull. I instinctively placed both my hands on my head to protect myself. Seeing that he was going to start hitting me again, I ran off to join the others in the queue. Our captors started hitting people as soon as we arrived; to vent their hatred, out of cruelty, and also so that we'd lose our bearings and obey out of fear, without making problems for them. So that's what I did, and when I turned around to try to find my mother, she wasn't there anymore. I never saw her again. She wasn't there, and neither were my two little sisters, Marica and Marta. . . .

How was the selection carried out?

As soon as we jumped out of the train, the Germans, with their whips and blows, made us get into two queues, sending the women and children to one side and all the men, without distinction, to the other. They beckoned us into place: "*Männer hier und Frauen hier!*" "Men here and women here!" We stepped into place like robots, in response to the yells and the orders.

How far away from the women were you? Could you still see them?

To begin with, we could, but the crowd very quickly became so dense, and at the same time so orderly, that I rapidly found myself surrounded only by men. Of all the men who'd been on that train, only three hundred and twenty of us were left after the selection.[1]

Everything happened relatively quickly. As I said, we didn't have any time to think. In situations like that, you feel as if you've lost your bearings, as if you're on another planet. The Germans had us encircled, with machine guns and dogs. Nobody could step out of line. I heard that some people had been given a blessing by their father or their mother. I'm happy for them. Unfortunately, not everybody was so lucky.

And did you at least manage to stay with your cousins?

Yes, we stayed together. I never saw their father or the others again.

They immediately made us all line up in front of a German officer. Another officer arrived shortly afterwards. I don't know if was the famous Dr. Mengele; it may have been, but I'm not sure. The officer barely looked at us and made a gesture with his thumb indicating *"Links, rechts!"* "Left, right!" and depending on the direction he sent us, each of us had to go one way or the other.

Did you notice any difference between the people who went to the right and those who went to the left?

No, I didn't notice: there were young men and old men on both sides. The only significant thing was the obvious imbalance between the numbers of people on both sides. I found

---

[1] The archives of the Auschwitz-Birkenau Museum indicate that, after the selection, out of the two thousand five hundred Jews deported at the same time as Shlomo, three hundred and twenty men entered the camp with identity numbers going from 182440 to 182759, and three hundred and twenty-eight women, given numbers from 76856 to 77183. All the others were immediately sent to their deaths in the gas chambers.

myself on the side where there were fewer people. In the end, there were just three hundred and twenty men left. All the others set off, without knowing it, for immediate death in the gas chambers at Birkenau. My brother and my cousins also ended up on the right side with me. Our group was sent on foot to Auschwitz I.[2]

In your view, how long did the process take, from arrival to the end of selection?

I think it lasted about two hours. Why do I think so? Because it was still daytime when we arrived on the *Judenrampe*, and the prisoners had already stopped working by the time my group reached Auschwitz I. We walked the distance, just over a mile or so, from the *Judenrampe* to the camp at Auschwitz I, while the others unsuspectingly headed off for the gas chambers at Birkenau.

I remember that, before entering the Auschwitz I main gate, with the inscription *"Arbeit macht frei,"* "Work makes free," I noticed a sign placed near the barbed-wire fence. It read: *"Vorsicht Hochspannung Lebensgefahr,"* meaning "Beware, high tension, danger of death."

Once inside, immediately on the left was block 24; we later discovered that it served as a brothel for the soldiers and a few privileged non-Jews. In the windows we could see pretty women laughing. I was told they weren't Jewish. I naïvely thought that, if there was a brothel, the camp itself must really be a place where people worked.

---

[2] Upon arrival almost all of the Jews selected for forced labor were sent to Birkenau. Some were occasionally sent straight to the camp at Auschwitz I or to the camp called Monowitz, which was Auschwitz III. It is likely that Shlomo Venezia's group was initially chosen to work in Auschwitz I, but after just a few hours, the labor service in the camp decided to transfer them to Birkenau.

Were you encircled and guarded by the SS when you went in?

Yes, all in all there must have been some ten or so soldiers; one every ten yards along our column. They accompanied us as far as the entrance, but once we were inside, they handed us on to the SS who were already inside the camp. When we went in, we saw, in the distance, prisoners who tried to come across to us and find out where we were from and if by any chance we had any news of their families. All at once, I heard a voice calling, "Shlomo! Shlomo!" Looking towards the prisoners, I spotted the fiancé of my sister Rachel, Aaron Mano, who was trying to attract my attention. He wanted to know if Rachel had been arrested too. I told him that, unfortunately, she had been deported with us, but I didn't know what had happened to her since.

Finally, the Germans ordered us to line up in groups of five in a narrow space between two blocks, opposite the kitchens. Here there were two Germans waiting for us, with a movie-camera. They told one of the prisoners who had been deported with us to go over so they could film him. I remember that man clearly, as he had the same family name as I, Venezia, Baruch Venezia, but he wasn't from my family. He was a very tall man, with the hooked nose and typical face of southern Jews. His features were tired and drawn after the journey. He hadn't shaved for several days; this, and his defeated expression, made him look even more miserable. I heard one of the Germans telling the other to film him, as he had a "perfect Jewish profile." These images were certainly used in Nazi propaganda to be shown in cinemas and thus spread a bad image of the Jews. At that moment, I realized we were in a place where we could expect only the worst. More than anything, I felt a surge of anger, of rage at having fallen so low, of being treated and humiliated like that. I would never have thought it possible. I also felt afraid, of course – we felt fear continually, whatever we did, since the worst could happen at any moment.

What happened when they made you line up?

We had to wait for an officer to come and give us instructions. We stood there motionless for a long time. Before the officer arrived, a Greek interpreter whom I knew from Salonika came over to us and warned us that the German was going to ask us a few questions. He advised us to answer without thinking twice, and to say that we were in good health, without any lice, and ready to work.

This man's name was Salvatore Cunio. He had a limp, and a man such as he certainly would have been sent to his death if he hadn't been able to speak German fluently. In fact, I soon realized that, in the camp, knowing foreign languages was a sometimes vital advantage. Cunio was married to a non-Jewish German woman; he had been deported with his son, Bubbi (his real name was Hans). He, too, was spared.

Finally, when the officer arrived, night had already fallen. He asked us the anticipated questions; we answered in the way the interpreter had indicated. Then the officer gave the order: "*Alle nach Birkenau!*" "Everyone to Birkenau!" So we turned around and set off for Birkenau. It was dark and there was a thick fog; one could see just a few lights in the distance. It must have been ten o'clock by the time we arrived in Birkenau.

We entered by the central tower, where the trains later started to come in. But, at the time of our arrival, the tracks leading right into the camp, designed to cope with the massive deportation of Hungarian Jews, were still under construction. The convoys continued to arrive at the *Judenrampe*, a few hundred yards from the entrance of Birkenau. Once I was in the camp, I don't know if we continued straight on, passing in front of Crematoria II and III[3] to come in from behind, or whether instead we passed down the Lagerstrasse.[4] Through the fog, all I could make out were the huts lit up by little lights on the right and left of the road. At the time, I didn't yet know who or what was in those buildings, so I didn't pay much attention.

We eventually entered the *Zentralsauna*,[5] a big brick structure used to disinfect people and clothes. The first thing we had to do was take off all our clothes. The same old problem of the "golden eggs" cropped up again. My brother, my cousins and I duly swallowed the coins for a second time.

At the far end of the first room we saw two doctors, SS officers in white coats. They watched as we walked naked in front of them. Every now and then they would motion to one of us to stay on the side. In this way they put some fifteen to eighteen people "on the side." Among them was a cousin of my father's. He had always seemed fragile and unhealthy. I wanted to know where they were going to be taken, so I asked a Greek man from Salonika who was working in the *Zentralsauna*. He told me that those people needed special care, and were going to be "treated." He certainly told me this so as not to worry

---

[3] In Auschwitz-Birkenau, the term "crematorium" (*Krematorium* in German) designates a structure including the room where the prisoners undressed, the gas chamber(s), and the crematorium ovens. There were four of these structures in Birkenau, in addition to the first crematorium situated at Auschwitz I. Crematoria II and III were built facing each other, as were Crematoria IV and V. They were brought into service between spring and summer of 1943. See the historical notes for more information, pp. 172–81.

[4] The main road running across the camp (see the plan in the central section).

[5] All the prisoners entering the camp had to go through disinfection and registration procedures. Until the end of 1943, these took place in two buildings situated inside sector BIa (for the women) and BIb (for the men) of Birkenau. From December 1943 onwards, the new building of the *Zentralsauna* was the main place for disinfecting and registering prisoners, both men and women.

me. I didn't ask any more questions, even if I didn't really understand what he'd meant. In reality, this was a second, "little" selection that we had unwittingly undergone. But the selection was superficial; you just needed buttocks that were a bit on the thin side to be condemned to death.

Those who hadn't been put aside continued on, and passed into the following room. In this room, "hairdressers" were lined up to shave our heads and entire bodies. Since they didn't have adequate tools, or any shaving foam, they pulled our skin off until we bled. In the following room were the showers. This was a big room with pipes and shower heads above us. A rather young German controlled the taps of hot and cold water. To amuse himself at our expense, he quickly changed from scalding hot to freezing cold water. The minute the water became too hot, we moved away so as not to get burned, and then he started howling like an animal, beat us and forced us to get back under the scalding water.

Everything happened in a highly organized way, like an assembly belt on which we were the finished products. As we stepped forward, others came to take our places. Still soaking wet and naked, I followed the queue until I reached the tattooing room. There was a long table at which several prisoners had been put to tattoo our identity numbers on our arms. They used a sort of ball-point pen with a sharp point that pierced one's skin and made the ink go in under the epidermis. They had to make these little penetrations until the number appeared on one's arm. It was extremely painful. When the man tattooing me finally dropped my arm, I immediately rubbed the front of my arm to lessen the pain. When I looked to see what he'd done to me, I couldn't make anything out under the mixture of blood and ink. I was suddenly frightened that I might have wiped the number out. With a bit of spit, I wiped my arm clean and I saw the number that had been correctly "injected": 182727, my identity.

After that, we had to wait for the clothes that were to be handed out to us. For some time now, new prisoners had not been given striped uniforms. Instead, we received disinfected clothes left by the prisoners who had arrived before us. They were handed out without anyone bothering to give us clothes that fit. We were given a jacket, a pair of trousers, underpants, shoes, and socks. The clothes were often frayed and full of holes. Several of the new arrivals couldn't get their trousers on, and others had been given trousers that were much too big. There was no way we could go and ask those who'd distributed the clothes for things of our own size. They might well have beaten us, even if they, too, were prisoners. So we tried to sort it out among ourselves by swapping clothes. But you needed to be lucky, especially with the shoes – so many of them had holes in their soles. I managed to get reasonable clothes, even if everything was a bit too large for me.

Since I was one of the first to be ready, and there were still a lot of men waiting behind me, I went over to one of the prisoners who were doing the shaving. I offered to assist him in exchange for a hunk of bread. The prisoner in charge of that work team agreed, and gave me a small pair of clippers. I knew how to use it – my father had a little barber's shop next to my grandfather's "Turkish" café. After my father's death, I'd earned a bit of money by going into the poor district in Baron Hirsch and offering my services to people who didn't have the means to pay for a proper hairdresser. This is the sort of thing that makes me often say that people who suffered in their childhood and had to learn to get by on their own had more of a chance of adapting to life in camp and surviving than did people from privileged backgrounds. To survive in the camp, you had to know things that were useful – not philosophy. That day's work enabled me to earn a precious hunk of bread.

So you didn't try to find out what had happened to your mother and your sisters?

Of course I tried. I never stopped thinking about my mother. I heard someone speaking Ladino, our Jewish-Spanish dialect, so I went over and asked him if he knew where they might have been sent. He gently told me not to worry, I'd know the next day, and meanwhile it was better not to ask myself too many questions. But this reply didn't satisfy me, so I went over to a prisoner who spoke Yiddish and asked him in German, *"Wo sind meine Mutter und meine Schwestern?"* "Where are my mother and my sisters?" He didn't reply, and just took me by the arm and led me to the window. From there, he pointed at the Crematorium chimney. I stared, disbelievingly, at what he was showing me and I realized he was telling me in Yiddish, "All the people who didn't come with you are already being freed from this place." I looked at him skeptically, without really believing him. We didn't exchange another word. I can't say I felt anything very much. It was so inconceivable that they would have brought us here just to burn us on arrival; I merely thought that he wanted to frighten me, as people do with rookies. So I decided to wait until the next day and to see for myself. But actually, he was all too correct.

How did you find your brother and your cousins?

Once I'd been given my clothes, I heard someone calling, "Shlomo? Where are you?" It was my brother calling me; I recognized his voice, but I couldn't see him. In fact, he was right next to me, but neither of us could recognize the other. We had no hair, and we were wearing ill-fitting clothes. It was a really sad moment, perhaps one of the saddest. To see the state we'd been reduced to. . . . But I didn't cry. Even when I found out about my mother. . . . The tap of my tears was blocked and I no longer cried, in spite of the sadness and the pain. . . .

When, eventually, the Germans made us leave the *Sauna*, they took us to a barrack opposite. It was completely empty; there was neither bed nor anything else on the ground. They put all of us in there until the following day, since at that time of night it was forbidden to move around in the camp. We stayed there, unable to sleep or stretch out; just like animals. Several of the religious boys started praying in a corner. They hadn't been able to keep their books, of course, but they knew the prayers by heart. The next morning, at nine o'clock, German guards came to take us to sector BIIa, the quarantine area in the men's camp.[6]

They pointed to a barrack, more or less in the middle of the quarantine sector, and told us to go in. The *Blockältester*,[7] a non-Jewish Pole who turned out to be particularly violent, was waiting for us. He ordered us to get into groups of five for each "bunk." I got together with my brother, my two cousins, and a friend from Salonika. At around eleven thirty the soup was distributed. This was the first time we'd received anything to eat since the Red Cross parcels. But in order to get the soup, one had to have a mess tin, and that wretched man hadn't bothered to tell us where to find one. What could we do? Anyone without a mess tin didn't get any soup and was roughly turned away. Nobody was bothered by the fact that we hadn't eaten for several days. They handed out a slice of black bread with a little margarine (sometimes, instead of

---

[6] The men's quarantine camp (*Quarantänelager für Männer*) was the only sector of the camp made up of a single row of huts. The Nazis set up the "quarantine" for all the prisoners brought into the camp so as to avoid introducing infectious diseases. If such epidemics were reported, the SS doctors solved the problem by sending all the prisoners from the contaminated hut to the gas chambers.

[7] Literally, the "oldest in the block." This term was generally employed to designate the man responsible for keeping order inside the huts. The term *Kapo* generally refers to the person in charge of a labor *Kommando*.

margarine, they'd give us a bit of what they called *Blutwurst*, a sort of sausage). I swallowed it all down in a single gulp, without even bothering to chew it, I was so hungry.

The next morning, they gave us some tea. Well, I'm not sure whether that filthy black water could be called water, tea, an infusion of linden leaves, or I don't know what, but at least it was hot. Anyway, as we still didn't have any mess tins, we didn't get any that time. Eventually someone showed me a place behind the quarantine block where I could find some mess tins. They were in such a state! Dirty, rusty, scattered all over the ground. But this didn't matter – the only thing that counted was that we could feed ourselves the minimum to survive until the following day. We needed to find some means of always keeping the mess tin on us; we made a hole in the wood to hook it onto our belts with a piece of string, any way we could. It was essential to keep these mess tins on us, since otherwise we risked having them stolen.

What did you do during the day?

Nothing particular. Prisoners had the right to move around within the quarantine sector. We could even talk with the other prisoners, not like in the Sonderkommando, where it was strictly forbidden to talk to anybody at all. The prisoners in quarantine did practically no work. In principle, you could talk to whomever you wanted. Except that the language barrier and the absence of any desire to go and recount our sufferings to people who were going through the same things as we were made us turn in on ourselves and take refuge in silence.

How did the roll call go?

It took place every day, morning and evening. They woke us up very early in the morning for roll call. Everyone out, with lots of shouts and beatings to get us outside as quickly as possible. The last were routinely punished and given an additional beating. But, inevitably, some had to be last, since we couldn't all of us get out at the same time. So everyone rushed to be the first out so as to avoid a thrashing. Roll call could last several hours, during which time we had to stand upright and motionless. After that, as we were still in quarantine and not in the labor kommandos, we were given the task of weeding, doing a bit of cleaning up – but nothing special. We could see the prisoners in the other sectors of the camp setting off to work.

What were the barracks in the quarantine area like?

The barracks had two entrances: one in front, the main entrance, and the other in the rear. When we went in, there were two little bedrooms on the right and the left, then the "bunks." In the middle was the stove, but it wasn't much use to us – I never saw it lit in the three weeks we spent in quarantine. And even if it had been lit, we didn't have any fuel to put into it to keep it working. The *Blockältester* had his own system for keeping warm, and was really not interested in knowing whether we were cold.

And the "bunks"?

I don't know if they can really be called "bunks". . . . We were put on three levels, with at least five people on each "bunk." Personally, I never had too many problems in keeping my place while we were in quarantine.

To begin with, we didn't know which were the best places. I soon realized that the places on top were too close to the windows. And the windows at Birkenau were often broken, which meant that, in winter, an icy wind blew in. But the bunks at the bottom weren't ideal, either. A lot of rather unpleasant things fell onto your head when the prisoners couldn't get up to go to the latrines. When there was a quarrel over who got which place, the kapo would barge in and sort out the problem, lashing out left, right, and center.

The one in charge of my barrack was a real shit. He was Polish. As far as I'm concerned, apart from the Sonderkommando, in which all the prisoners, or almost all, were Jewish (including the kapo), I never saw any Jewish kapos, neither in Auschwitz nor in the other camps I was in subsequently. It's possible there were some, but I myself only ever saw Germans, Poles, and even Frenchmen – but none of them was Jewish.

The kapo generally coordinated the labor teams. Sometimes, the *Blockältester* was also called the kapo. If he wasn't able to hurry the work along, he hit out, and if he didn't hit out often enough or hard enough, the Germans killed that kapo and chose another one. But some kapos enjoyed the privilege of being personally able to kill prisoners in their charge. The SS often chose German criminals, who all at once took themselves for the masters of the world. They should have been locked away in a cell but, instead of that, they were in a position of power over us. So the Germans didn't need guards everywhere. They could rely on those violent men to maintain discipline in the camp. If they weren't violent, they risked losing their privileges, and that's why all of us were frightened of them.

Do you remember any names?

No, unfortunately I've forgotten, since I didn't pay any attention to their names. If I'd known that one day I'd emerge from that hell, I'd have made a note of all the names, the dates, and the details. But while we were there, we didn't even know what day it was.

The Kapo I had in quarantine was in fact the *Blockältester*. He was a particularly brutal man. He had his room at the entrance to the barrack. Opposite, another little room served either as a lumber room, or as a bedroom for the *Pipel*. The *Pipel* was a young boy, generally about twelve years old, whom the *Blockältester* always kept near to him. He was the *Blockältester*'s jack-of-all-trades and had to obey all his orders and fulfill all his wishes. He polished his shoes, cleaned the barrack, made his bed, and also had to satisfy his unwholesome desires when the kapo demanded. The youngster knew that if he were dismissed he'd be heading for certain death, so he had no choice but to obey. In exchange, he had a little more to eat than the others. The *Blockältester* just needed to give a bit less to one prisoner so he could give more to those whom he favored.

I almost got onto the wrong side of him, on one occasion. It had to do with those "golden eggs" of ours. It hadn't been easy to get hold of them again after the *Zentralsauna* – in quarantine, the latrine barracks were just a long wooden bench with holes in it. It would have been impossible to fish anything out of there. So I needed to find a place that was safe from prying eyes. We'd take turns going to the toilet, while the others stood guard. One day, the kapo summoned me and demanded that I give him my gold coins, "*die goldene Geld*," as he called it. I pretended I didn't know what he was talking about. But he insisted: "*Fünf goldene Geld!*" "Five gold coins!" If he knew the exact number of coins, someone must have told him; he hadn't made it up by himself. I even found out later who had betrayed us. Meanwhile, the kapo told me that I had twenty-four hours to bring him the coins. I went to see my brother and my cousins, and I told them what had happened. Their opinion was that I should hand them over, as they thought it was pointless to risk getting killed as well as losing the money. So I went to see him, but I claimed I had only three of the five left. He replied, very angrily, "*Nein! Fünf!*" My life was in his hands, I had no choice – so I went to get the two last coins, in exchange for which he did in fact promise me a double ration of soup and bread for a week. He got what he wanted and, indeed, on the first two days, he did give me a double ration. But on the third day. . . .

With that money, he'd managed to get his hands on some sausage and vodka. He organized a little party for himself, and got really drunk. One evening, while all of us were in bed, he started yelling, "*Auf die Tür!*"; he wanted someone to open the door to his room. He chose someone at random, gave the victim a few kicks without any reason, and ordered him to go to the door and open it. The poor boy went without knowing what to expect. But just as the youngster put his hand onto the door handle, he got a big electric shock. The *Blockältester* started to laugh, since it was his favorite hobby to make us suffer, especially when he was drunk. He chose another prisoner so as to play the practical joke once again. The poor man knew what to expect, but had no choice, and got up. He grasped the door handle and opened the door quite normally, without anything happening. The Pole grew angry when he saw that his joke had stopped working. He ordered the prisoner to open the door again. He opened it, shut it; still nothing happened. The *Blockältester* took a minute or two to realize that the wooden clogs the prisoner was wearing insulated him from the earth. So he ordered the man to take off his clogs and open the door again. This time, when the man touched the handle, he in turn got an electric shock, to the great amusement of our tormentor. While he was getting ready to choose a new victim, the door to the barrack opened and in stormed an SS man, furious. The time for lights out in the barrack had already passed and he'd come to see why the rule wasn't being obeyed. He immediately started yelling. The *Blockältester* tried to explain by saying it was his birthday. He invited the German to share the feast that my gold coins had paid for. The

German went up, opened the door, and duly got an electric shock. He was enraged, and started beating the *Blockältester*. How dare he play a practical trick on a German! He gave him a real thrashing. The next day this *Blockältester* had vanished, and we never saw him again. The downside of it all for me was that I'd missed out on the several remaining days of double ration he owed me. That's how the story of the "golden eggs" ended.

There was another experience that left its mark on me while I was in quarantine. This happened just a few days after our arrival. A kapo came to see us and told us that, if we were willing to do some extra work, he'd give us a double ration of soup. We all wanted to go, since hunger was stronger than anything. I found myself among the ten people chosen to do the job. But neither my brother nor my cousins were in the group. The kapo made us take a cart like the ones used to transport hay. But instead of horses, we were the ones who had to pull the cart. We dragged it to a barrack at the far end of the quarantine sector. It was called the *Leichenkeller*: the room of the corpses. When we opened the door, a terrible smell grabbed us by the throat; it was the stench of rotting bodies.

I'd never been past this barrack before, and this was how I found out that it was used to store the bodies of detainees who had died in quarantine. A small group of prisoners came into the barracks every morning to remove the bodies of prisoners who had died during the night. They were placed in this barrack before being taken to the Crematorium to be burned. The corpses sometimes stayed there, rotting, for two to three weeks. Those at the back were already in an advanced state of decomposition because of the heat.

If I'd known that our "extra" work was going to consist of bringing these bodies out and taking them to the Crematorium, I'd rather have died of hunger. But by the time I realized, it was already too late. There must have been a hundred or a hundred and twenty bodies in the room. We had to make three journeys there and back to carry them on the cart.

When we arrived in front of the gate of Crematorium III, the kapo had to ring for the men in the Sonderkommando to fetch the cart full of corpses. Other than they, none of the prisoners could enter the Crematorium and come out alive. So they emptied the cart themselves before giving it back to us.

Were you able to see anything? The inner court? The building?

No, that day I didn't see anything of the Crematorium. They hardly opened the gate. All we could see was the man opening the gate and taking the cart, with three other prisoners from inside. I'd heard that those who worked in the Crematorium were sometimes able to get extra spoons or other things that would be of use in the camp. So the second time I went there, I discreetly asked the man who'd opened the gate whether he might have a spoon he could give me. "*Nicht jetzt, später!*" "Not now, later!" And the third time I went, he did indeed give me two spoons. I gave one to my brother, but we shared them with my cousins. They were very useful for scraping the bottom of the mess tin and not wasting a single vital calorie of the food we were given. Eating with a spoon gave the impression we had more to eat.

Luckily, we didn't have to do that terrible job again. The next day, when it was time for soup, the kapo served us a double ration, as promised.

What did you know about the place where the corpses were taken?

I knew it was the Crematorium. I already knew at the time what that meant. While we were in quarantine, we constantly saw the smoke emerging from the chimney, and it was impossible to escape from the acrid smell of burnt flesh that drifted through the whole camp. I soon knew that it was the place where the bodies were burned, but it was only when I actually worked in the Crematorium that I realized it was also the place where people were gassed en masse when they arrived.

How were you selected for the Sonderkommando?

We spent three weeks in quarantine. Then, one day, we saw some German officers arriving. We didn't often see Germans in the quarantine sector; in general, it was the kapos who maintained order. These officers stopped in front of our barrack and ordered the kapo to get us to line up, as if for roll call. Each of us had to say what kind of job he was able to do. Even if we didn't have a trade or profession, everyone knew that he had to lie. When my turn came, I said I was a hairdresser. Leon Cohen, a Greek friend who always stayed close to us, said that he was a dentist, even though he'd actually worked at a bank. He thought they'd put him in a dental surgery to do some cleaning and polishing, and that way at least he'd stay nice and warm. I thought that I'd join the prisoners working in the *Zentralsauna*. I saw that the work wasn't too difficult and one was warm there. But in fact things didn't work out at all the way we'd expected. The Germans chose eighty people, including myself, my brother, and my cousins.

The next day, at around nine o'clock, we lined up and set off to sector BIId (*Lager d*).[8] This was the men's sector in Birkenau. The first impression I had when I entered *Lager d* was intensely unpleasant. Our group first went through the SS barrack, which was situated at the entrance to every sector to keep note of who entered and left the camp. After the barrack, on the right, I immediately spotted the pool filled with water. Then my eyes rose to the gallows that had been erected at one

[8] See historical note, p. 176.

corner of the pool. This vision had a profound effect on me; I
said to myself, "What a fine welcome they're giving us!"

Lager d consisted of two rows of barracks. The first two
buildings, bigger than the others, were used as the kitchens. In the middle of all those huts was that of the
Sonderkommando.[9] When I went in, I saw a prisoner, by himself, who seemed to be waiting for us. I don't know why he
came over to me, but anyway, he asked me affably, "*Retst
Yiddish?*" "Do you speak Yiddish?" I'd never heard Yiddish in
Greece, but since I'd been in the camp, I'd had to adapt, and
thanks to the little bit of German that I'd learned by trading
on the black market with the soldiers, I managed to speak
"yiddish, yaddish, yoddish." We finally managed to understand each other! He asked me where I was from, and if I were
hungry. After the prison in Athens, the eleven-day journey,
and the three weeks in quarantine, I'd been tightening my belt
now for a month and a half, so much that I could hardly
breathe. Of course I was hungry! I'd always been familiar with
hunger, but this was now an obsession, an illness. So he went
to get me some food and came back with a big hunk of white
bread and some jam. There was enough bread for me to share
it with my brother and my cousins. For us, it was like eating
caviar; an unimaginable luxury in this hell. He asked me if I
knew what the job would involve. I replied that I didn't much
care. As far as I was concerned, the main thing was being able
to eat and so survive. He told me that wouldn't be a problem
– there'd be enough to eat. I was a little puzzled by this: how
could it be possible in such a place for there to be "enough" to
eat? He explained that, in addition to the food we received in
the normal course of affairs, there would be other things. But

---

[9] The Sonderkommando barrack was block II of the men's camp (BIId).
With hut 13 (that of the *Strafkompanie*, the punishment company), from
which it was separated by the latrine hut, the Sonderkommando barrack
was isolated from the rest.

he didn't tell me what, or how. Then he asked me if I knew the name of the Kommando to which we had been assigned. Since I didn't have the slightest idea, he told me we were in the "Sonderkommando."

"What does 'Sonderkommando' mean?"

"Special detachment."

"Special? Why?"

"Because you have to work in the Crematorium . . . where the people are burned."

As far as I was concerned, one job was the same as any other; I'd already got used to camp life. But at no time did he tell me that the corpses to be burned were those of people who were still alive when they entered the Crematorium. . . .

He also told me that all the people in the Sonderkommando were regularly "selected" and "transferred" to another place. This happened about every three months. For the time being, I didn't realize that the words "selection" and "transfer" were euphemisms that actually meant "elimination." But it didn't take me long to realize that we had been incorporated into the Sonderkommando to replace former prisoners who had been "selected" and killed.[10]

This man was named Avraham Dragon. Actually, it was only when I saw him again sixty years later, in Israel, that I found out what his name was. I told him this story, with the vague hope that he might be the person who had given me such a humane reception, and whom I had never seen since. He smiled at me; he was moved, and said that he had never forgotten the famished young Greek who had landed in the Sonderkommando.

[10] On February 20, 1944, two hundred members of the Sonderkommando were sent to the camp of Lublin-Majdanek to be eliminated.

3

SONDERKOMMANDO: INITIATION

The barrack of the Sonderkommando was similar to all the others, apart from the fact that it was surrounded by barbed-wire fences and a brick wall that isolated us from the other barracks in the men's camp. We couldn't communicate with the other prisoners. But we didn't stay there for long. After about a week we were transferred into the dormitory right inside the Crematorium. It was only towards the end, when the crematoria were dismantled, that the Sonderkommando men came back to sleep in the barrack in the men's camp.

On the first day, they sent us to the Crematorium, but we stayed in the courtyard, without going into the building. At that time, we called it Crematorium I, since we were unaware of the existence of the first crematorium, in Auschwitz I.[1] There were three steps leading inside the building but, instead of going in, the kapo took us all round it. One of the Sonderkommando men came to tell us what to do: remove the

[1] For more information, see the historical note, p. 172.

weeds and tidy up the ground a bit. What we did wasn't particularly useful, but I suppose that the Germans wanted to keep us busy before making us work in the Crematorium. The next day, we came back to do the same thing.

My natural curiosity impelled me to go up to the building to try to see through the window what was going on inside. We had been strictly forbidden to do so, but, step by step, I edged up to the window. When I got close enough to catch a glimpse, I was left completely paralyzed by what I saw. Bodies heaped up, thrown on top of one another, were just lying there. These were the corpses of people who were still young. I came back to my companions and told them what I'd seen. They in turn slipped over to see, without the kapo noticing. They came back ashen-faced, disbelieving. We didn't dare think about what might have happened. It was only later that I realized that the corpses were the "leftovers" from an earlier convoy. There hadn't been time to burn them before the new convoy arrived, and these bodies were piled there to leave room in the gas chamber.

At around two in the afternoon the kapo made us go down into the undressing room. The floor was strewn with clothes of every sort. We'd been ordered to use the jackets and shirts to roll the clothes up into little bundles. Then we had to take the bundles and pile them up outside, in front of the stairs. I imagine a truck then came to pick up the packets to take them to the barracks in the Kanada.[2]

At around five the kapo again ordered us to assemble. We obviously assumed that, at this time in the evening, "assembly" meant we'd finished that laborious day's work. But unfortunately this wasn't the case. We came back out of the Crematorium, but instead of turning right to go back to the

---

[2] This was a sector inside the Birkenau camp in which objects belonging to the deported Jews were sorted through and stored; the Nazis called it *Effektenlager* or *Kanada II*.

"Bunker 2. Previous farm building transformed into gas chamber,"
David Olère, 1945. Wash and China ink on paper. Yad Vashem,
Jerusalem, Israel

barracks, they made us turn left, through the little forest of birches. I'd never seen this kind of tree in Greece, but in Birkenau they were the only trees one saw surrounding the camp. As we walked along the path, all we could hear was the wind whistling through the silvery leaves. All of a sudden, murmurs started to reach us from behind. To begin with, the noise was very faint and faraway. We came to a little house called, as I later learned, Bunker 2, or "the white house." Just then, the murmuring of human voices became more intense.

Can you describe Bunker 2 as you saw it?

It was a small farm with a thatched roof. We were ordered to stand opposite one side of the little house, near the road that ran in front of it. From where we were, we could see nothing,

neither on the left nor the right. Dusk was falling; the murmurs had become the distinct sound of people coming
towards us. I was curious, as usual, and went across to try to
see what was happening. I saw entire families waiting in front
of the cottage: young men, women, and children. There must
have been two or three hundred of them altogether. I don't
know where they'd come from, but I suppose they'd been
deported from a Polish ghetto. Later on, when I realized the
way the extermination system worked, I deduced that these
people had been sent to Bunker 2 because the other crematoria were full. This was also why they needed a bigger labor
force to do this dirty work.

Did people get undressed in front of the door or in a barrack?

People were forced to get undressed where they were, in front
of the door. The children were crying. You could feel the fear
and dread; people were really helpless and terrified. The
Germans probably had told them they'd be taking a shower
and then they'd been given something to eat. Even if they'd
realized what was really going to happen, there wasn't much
they could do; the Germans would have executed on the spot
anyone who'd made the least attempt to escape. They'd lost
all respect for the human person, but they knew that if they
left families together they would avoid having to deal with any
acts of desperation.

Finally the people were forced to enter the little house. The
door was closed. Once everyone was inside, a little truck, with
the Red Cross sign on its sides, drove up. A rather tall German
got out. He went over to a small opening high up on one of
the walls of the little house. He had to climb onto a stool to
reach it. He took a can, opened it, and threw the contents in
through the little opening. Then he closed the opening
and left. The shouts and crying had not stopped, and they

redoubled in intensity after a few minutes. This lasted for ten or twelve minutes, then silence.

Meanwhile, we'd been ordered to go around to the back of the house. When we arrived, I noticed a strange gleam coming from that direction. As I went over, I realized that the light was that of a fire burning in the ditches some twenty yards away.

Do you remember what you thought when you saw all that?

It's difficult to imagine now, but we didn't think of anything – we couldn't exchange a single word. Not because it was forbidden, but because we were terror-struck. We had turned into robots, obeying orders while trying not to think, so we could survive for a few hours longer. Birkenau was a real hell; nobody can understand or grasp the logic of that camp. That's why I want to tell the story, tell it for as long as I live, but relying only on my memories, on what I am certain that I saw, and nothing else.

So the Germans sent us to the other side of the house, where the ditches were. They ordered us to bring the bodies out of the gas chamber and place them in front of the ditches. I didn't go into the gas chamber myself; I stayed outside, going back and forth between the Bunker and the ditches. Other men from the Sonderkommando, more experienced than we were, had the job of laying the bodies out in the ditches in such a way that the fire wouldn't go out. If the bodies were packed in too densely, the air couldn't get through and there was a risk that the fire would go out or fade in intensity. That would have made the kapos and the Germans overseeing us furious. The ditches sloped down, so that, as they burned, the bodies discharged a flow of human fat down the ditch to a corner where a sort of basin had been formed to collect it. When it looked as if the fire might go out, the men had to take some of that liquid fat from the basin, and throw it onto the fire to revive the flames. I saw this only in the ditches of Bunker 2.

After two hours of this particularly taxing and distressing work, we heard the roar of a motorbike. The old hands murmured with terror: "*Malahamoves!*" That's when we made the macabre acquaintance of the "Angel of Death." That was the Yiddish name given by the prisoners to the dreaded SS man named Moll.[3] A single glance from him made you tremble. It didn't take long for us to discover his cruelty and the sadistic pleasure with which he mistreated us. No sooner had he put his foot onto the ground than he started to shout like an enraged beast, "*Arbeit!*" "Get working, pigs – *Schweine* – Jews!" Everyone started working harder when he arrived. When he realized that it was taking two of us to carry a dead body, he lost his temper and started yelling, "*Nein! Nur eine Person für einen Toten!*" "Only one person for one dead person!" It was difficult enough for two people to carry a corpse on the muddy ground into which our feet kept sinking. But do it alone! I don't know how I managed; I felt exhausted.

At a given moment, I saw one of the men holding a corpse come to a halt. He stood still. He must have been a few years older than I, barely twenty-five or so. Everyone walking past him, between the Bunker and the ditches, urged him to get moving before Moll noticed him. But he didn't reply, and went on standing there, gazing into the infinite distance. When Moll saw him, he went up to him, yelling, "*Du verfluchter Jude!*" "You cursed Jew! Why aren't you working, you Jewish dog? Get a move on!" And he started lashing him with

---

[3] SS-Hauptscharführer Otto Moll entered Birkenau to run Bunkers 1 and 2. He spent some time as Lagerführer in the subsidiary camps of Fürstengrube and Gleiwitz I, before being recalled to Birkenau in May 1944, where he stayed until September; he was in charge of all the crematoria. He was later transferred to Dachau. On December 13, 1945, Moll was sentenced to death at the Dachau trials. He was hanged in the Landsberg prison on May 28, 1946.

his whip. But the man just stood there, motionless, as if nothing could affect him anymore; he didn't even attempt to ward off the blows. In my opinion, he'd completely lost his wits; his mind was no longer of this world. He no longer seemed to feel either pain or fear. The German, furious at the offense committed and the lack of any reaction to his blows, pulled a pistol from his belt. We just continued coming and going. We saw him take aim and fire from a distance of a few yards. But, as if the bullet hadn't hit him, the man continued to stand there, motionless. How was it he hadn't dropped dead after that fatal shot? We didn't know what to think. The German, increasingly agitated, fired a second shot from the same pistol. But still no reaction; the bullets, the noise, the fear – nothing seemed to affect him. We thought it must be a miracle, but a miracle that could not last forever. I happened to be next to Moll when I saw him putting away his pistol and taking out another, bigger-caliber one. He fired a shot and the poor man fell dead. I had the misfortune to be near the body just then. I was returning from the ditch, empty-handed, to fetch another corpse. Moll motioned me towards him. *"Du! Komm her!"* "Come here!" He ordered me and another prisoner to carry the body to the ditches. We'd gone barely a few yards when he started yelling, as if he'd just thought of something. *"Halt!!! Ausziehen!"* He said the clothes belonged to the Third Reich and couldn't be burned with the dead man; they could be used for other prisoners. He ordered us to undress him. To undress a dead body that was still warm, a man whom we knew. . . . But of course, I had no choice if I was to avoid the same fate as this poor man. We didn't know what to think; we were outside the world, already in hell. When his body was thrown in the ditch, we saw the burning embers leaping up – it was like when you throw a piece of wood onto a fire in the grate, the flames suddenly roar up as if to devour the body more effectively. Until that point I'd more or less forbidden myself to think about everything that was happening; we had to do what we were ordered to do, like robots, without thinking. But on seeing the body burning I thought the dead were perhaps luckier than the living; they were no longer forced to endure this hell on earth, to see the cruelty of men.

Work went on like this until the following morning. We worked practically without stopping for twenty-four hours before they would give us permission to go back to our barracks. But in spite of my intense exhaustion, I didn't manage to get to sleep. The images just kept on haunting me, and the idea of returning to that place made me edgy. In the afternoon, a kapo came to tell us that the men who'd worked at Bunker 2 the night before didn't need to go back that night. Small consolation. . . .

The respite didn't last. The very next day, we had to set off to work again. I was sent to Crematorium III with a little group of about fifteen people. As I'd said that I was a hairdresser, the *Oberkapo* who'd met us when we arrived at the Crematorium placed in my hands a pair of very long scissors, like the ones used by tailors to cut fabric. Then they directed us towards the room in which we were supposed to be working. The old hands very succinctly explained to us what we needed to do.

The contact with the dead was immediate. The deportees of a previous convoy had just been gassed and the men in the Sonderkommando were already busy taking the corpses out of the gas chamber. They were laid out in a kind of atrium, before being taken up to the Crematorium ovens. This was where I had to cut off the hair of the dead bodies. There were three or four of us doing this job. Then two "dentists" came along to extract the victims' gold teeth, which they kept in a special little container that nobody could go near. One of them was my friend Leon Cohen, who'd claimed he was a dentist. They gave him a dentist's forceps and a little mirror

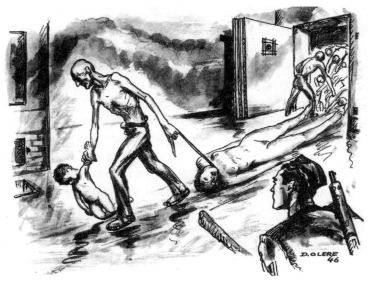

"After the gassing," David Olère, 1946. Wash and China ink on paper. Ghetto Fighters Museum, Galilee, Israel

to see inside the mouth. I remember that, when he realized what it was he was supposed to do, he almost fainted. To begin with, when he worked on the first corpses, he went quite quickly, he opened their mouths and removed the gold teeth. But as he continued, it all became more difficult, since the corpses had had time to stiffen, and he had to force their jaws open.

What did you see of the gas chamber when you arrived?

I wasn't one of those who had to take the corpses out of the gas chamber, but later on I frequently had to do it. Those given this task started by pulling the corpses out with their hands, but in a few minutes their hands were dirty and slippery. In order to avoid touching the bodies directly, they tried using a bit of cloth, but, of course, the cloth in turn became dirty and damp after a few moments. So people had to make do. Some tried to drag the bodies along with a belt, but this actually made the work even harder, since they had to keep tying and untying the belt. Finally, the simplest thing was to use a walking stick under the nape of the neck to pull the bodies along. You can see it very clearly in one of David Olère's drawings.[4] There was no shortage of walking sticks, because of all the elderly people who were put to death. At least this meant we didn't have to drag the corpses with our hands. And this was hugely important for us. Not because it was a matter of corpses, though that was bad enough. . . . It was because their death had been anything but gentle. It was a foul, filthy death. A forced death, difficult and experienced differently by each of them.

I've never talked about this until now; it's such a weight, it's so heartrending, that I find it difficult to speak of those visions of the gas chamber. You could find people whose eyes hung out of their sockets because of the struggles the organism had undergone. Others were bleeding from everywhere, or were soiled by their own excrement, or that of other people. Because of the effect that their fear and the gas had on them, the victims often evacuated everything they had in their bodies. Some bodies were all red, others very pale, as everyone reacted differently. But they had all suffered in death. People often imagine that the gas was thrown in, and there you were, the victims died. But what a death it was! . . . You

---

[4] David Olère, a Jewish-French painter of Polish origin, was deported from France in March 1943. He was taken to Auschwitz-Birkenau, where he was assigned to the Sonderkommando of Crematorium III. He was, like Shlomo, one of the few survivors of these special Kommandos. His drawings were made shortly after the Liberation and are an exceptional visual testimony to the extermination process in the gas chambers. With the kind permission of his son Alexandre Oler, some of David's drawings are reproduced here, illustrating Shlomo Venezia's words. See also the historical note "About David Olère" at the end of this volume.

"Crematorium III fully operational," David Olère, 1945. Wash and China ink on paper. Ghetto Fighters Museum, Galilee, Israel

found them gripping each other – everyone had desperately sought a little air. The gas was thrown onto the floor and gave off acid from underneath, so everyone tried to find some air, even if each one needed to climb on top of another until the last one died. I personally think – I can't be sure but I think – that several people died even before the gas was thrown in. They were crammed in so tightly against one another that the smallest and weakest were inevitably suffocated. At a certain moment, under that pressure, that anguish, you become selfish and there's only one thing you can think of: how to save yourself. That was the effect the gas had. The sight that lay before us when we opened the door was terrible; nobody can even imagine what it was like.

During the first days, in spite of the hunger that was tormenting my belly, I found it hard to touch the hunk of bread we were given. The stench stuck to my hands; I felt sullied by those deaths. With time, little by little, we had to get used to everything. It became a kind of routine that we couldn't think about.

*"In the undressing room," David Olère, 1946. Wash and China ink on
paper. Ghetto Fighters Museum, Galilee, Israel*

*Can you describe in detail what happened when each new convoy
arrived?*

Every time a new convoy arrived, people went in through the
big door of the Crematorium and were directed towards the
underground staircase that led to the undressing room. There
were so many of them that we saw the queue stretching out
like a long snake. As the first of them were entering, the last
were still a hundred yards or so behind. After the selection on
the ramp, the women, children, and old men were sent in first,
then the other men arrived. In the undressing room, there
were coat hooks with numbers all along the wall, as well as
little wooden planks on which people could sit to get
undressed. To deceive them more effectively, the Germans
told people to pay particular attention to the numbers, so that
they'd be able to find their things more easily when they came
out of the "shower." After a time, they also added an instruc-
tion to use the laces to tie shoes in pairs. In fact, this was to

facilitate the process of sorting out when the things arrived at the *Kanadakommando*. These instructions were generally given by the SS standing guard, but it sometimes happened that a man in the Sonderkommando could speak the language of the deportees and transmit these instructions to them directly. To calm people down and ensure they'd go through more quickly, without making any fuss, the Germans also promised them they'd have a meal just after "disinfection." Many of the women hurried up so as to be first in line and get it all over with as quickly as possible – especially as the children were terrified and clung to their mothers. For them, even more than for the others, everything must have been strange, eerie, dark, cold.

Once they had taken off their clothes, the women went into the gas chamber and waited, thinking that they were in a shower, with the shower heads hanging over them. They couldn't know where they really were. A woman would sometimes be seized by doubt when no water came out and went to see one of the two Germans outside the door. She was immediately beaten and forced to go back in; that took away any desire she might have to ask questions.

Then the men, too, were finally pushed into the gas chamber. The Germans thought that if they made thirty or so strong men go in last, they would be able, with their force, to push the others right in. And indeed, herded by the rain of blows as if they were so many animals, their only option was to push hard to get into the room to avoid the beating. That's why I think that many of them were dead or dying even before the gas was released. The German whose job it was to control the whole process often enjoyed making these people, who were about to die, suffer a bit more. While waiting for the arrival of the SS man who was going to release the gas, he amused himself by switching the light on and off to frighten them a little more. When he switched off the light, you could

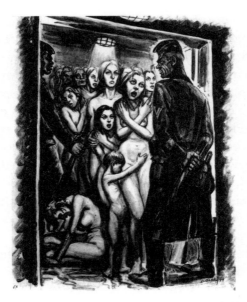

*"In the gas chamber," David Olère, 1950. Wash and China ink on
paper. Private collection*

hear a different sound emerging from the gas chamber; the
people seemed to be suffocating with anguish, they'd realized
they were going to die. Then he'd switch the light back on and
you heard a sort of sigh of relief, as if the people thought the
operation had been canceled.

Then, finally, the German bringing the gas would arrive.
It took two prisoners from the Sonderkommando to help
him lift up the external trapdoor, above the gas chamber,
then he introduced Zyklon B through the opening. The lid
was made of very heavy cement. The German would never
have bothered to lift it up himself, as it needed two of us.
Sometimes it was me, sometimes others. I've never said this
before, since it's painful to admit that we had to lift the lid
and put it back, once the gas had been introduced. But that's
how it was.

Did the SS man wear a gas mask?

No, I never saw a German wearing one, neither when pouring the gas in nor when opening the door. I know many people have claimed they did wear them. That may have been the case in other crematoria, but in any case not in mine. There was no point, since the operation was very rapid. The cover was just opened, the gas thrown in, and the cover closed again. But the German merely threw the gas in; it wasn't even he who opened or closed.

Once the gas had been thrown in, it lasted about ten to twelve minutes, then finally you couldn't hear anything anymore, not a living soul. A German came to check that everyone was really dead by looking through a peephole placed in the thick door (it had iron bars on the inside to prevent the victims from trying to smash the glass). When he was sure that everyone was well and truly dead, he opened the door and came out right away, after starting the ventilation system. For twenty minutes, you could hear a loud throbbing noise, like a machine breathing in air. Then, finally, we could go in and start to bring the corpses out of the gas chamber. A terrible, acrid smell filled the room. We couldn't distinguish between what came from the specific smell of the gas and what came from the smell of the people and the human excrement.

What were you supposed to do, exactly?

I was given scissors and had to cut off the women's hair. I just cut off the longest hair, and didn't touch the men. Especially useful were the long tresses, easy to cut off and transport. Both hands were needed to cut with those big pairs of scissors. Then the hair was picked up and put into a big sack. At regular intervals, a truck came to pick up the sacks of hair that had

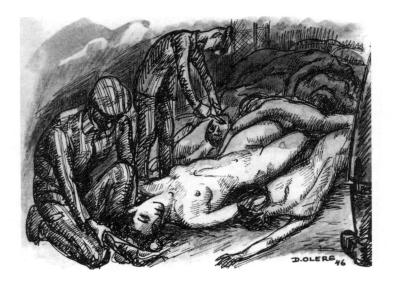

"Our hair, our teeth, and our ashes," David Olère, 1946. Wash and China ink on paper. Yad Vashem, Jerusalem, Israel

been set to one side so as to convey them to a place in town where they were stored.

When the job of cutting the hair and pulling out the gold teeth had been completed, two people came to take the bodies and to load them onto the hoist that sent them up to the ground floor of the building, and the Crematorium ovens. All the rest, the undressing room and the gas chamber, was underground. Depending on whether the people were big, small, fat, or thin, it was possible to load between seven and ten people onto the hoist. On the floor above, two people collected the bodies and sent the lift back down. The hoist didn't have any door; a wall blocked the one side, but when they reached floor level, the corpses were unloaded on the other side. The bodies were then dragged and laid out in front of the ovens, two by two.

In front of every muffle, three men were waiting to place

the bodies in the oven. The bodies were laid out head to foot on a kind of stretcher. Two men, either side of the stretcher, lifted it with the help of a long piece of wood slipped underneath it. The third man, facing the ovens, held the handles that were used to push the stretcher into the furnace. They had to slip the bodies in and pull the stretcher out quickly, before the iron grew too hot. The men in the Sonderkommando had got into the habit of pouring water onto the stretcher before disposing of the bodies, otherwise these remained stuck to the red-hot iron. In cases such as that, the work became very difficult, since the bodies had to be pulled out with a fork and pieces of skin remained attached. When this happened, the whole process was slowed down and the Germans could accuse us of sabotage. So we had to move quickly and skillfully.

In David Olère's drawings, you can see a strip of water in front of the ovens . . .

This was mainly used to transport the bodies more easily between the hoist and the ovens. Water was thrown into this channel and the bodies slipped along relatively easily. Not like in Bunker 2, where our feet, and the bodies too, got bogged down in the mud. To bring the bodies out of the gas chamber, there was no need to water the ground, since it was already sufficiently moist with everything – and I mean absolutely everything: blood, excrement, urine, vomit, everything. . . . Sometimes we slipped up in it.

I said that in general, I cut the hair, but I sometimes worked in the gas chamber, to help out a friend who was exhausted. My work was a little less demanding and I agreed to swap over with him, to give him time to rest or get a bit of fresh air. The worst of it was at the beginning, when we had to pull out the first bodies, since we didn't have anything to help us. The

"In the oven room," David Olère, 1945. Wash and China ink on paper.
Ghetto Fighters Museum, Galilee, Israel

bodies were so entangled and twisted together – legs here, heads there. The bodies lay in a pile more than three feet high, sometimes four feet or more.

Once the room had been emptied, it had to be thoroughly cleaned, since the walls and the floor were all dirty, and it was impossible to get new people in without their panicking at the sight of the traces of blood and all the rest on the walls and on the ground. We first had to clean the floor, wait for it to dry and then whitewash the walls. The ventilator continued to clean the air. Thus, everything was ready for the arrival of a new group. Even if people saw the floor was wet when they came in, this didn't strike them as being suspicious, since they'd been told that they'd be going into the shower to be disinfected.

So, all traces were effaced in the gas chamber. And in the ovens, what happened with the ashes, once the bodies had been burned?

The ashes had to be eliminated too, so as to leave no trace. In fact, certain bones, those of the pelvis, for instance, didn't burn very well, either in the ovens or, indeed, in the ditches. That's why the thickest bones had to be taken out and ground up separately, before being mixed with the ashes. The operation took place in the Crematorium yard, behind the building. In Crematorium III, for example, the place where the bones were ground was in the corner next to the hospital and the Gypsy camp. Once the ashes had all been ground up, they were transported on the back of a little wagon. At regular intervals, a truck came to collect them so they could be thrown into the river. Sometimes I would swap places with one of the men who had to grind up the bones. This enabled me to get a bit of fresh air and escape from the oppressive, fetid atmosphere of the Crematorium.

Did the process of gassing and cremation ever stop?

No, we worked in two shifts, a day shift and a night shift, but the work was meant never to stop. It was a continuous, uninterrupted process. Just once we were forced to stop for two days because of a problem in the chimney. Because they had been overheated, some bricks had melted, which had obstructed the air passage. For the Germans, losing two days' work was a real tragedy. A young Polish Jew, covered with sacks to protect himself against the soot and the heat, opened the base (the foundation) of the chimney so he could extract the bricks that were causing the problem. I noticed the bricks were glistening, encrusted with human grease. Because of this two-day interruption, resuming work on the last three hundred corpses was particularly hard. In the heat, they had decomposed. But they hadn't stiffened, as happens with people who die a natural death: the gassed bodies disintegrated. I tried to pull a body out, but the skin came off in pieces and stuck to my hands. It was terrible.

So work resumed immediately when a new group arrived. And what did you do while the people were in the undressing room?

In general, I would rest until I had to start my "work." But sometimes, too, I ended up in the room, helping out so that everything would happen as calmly as possible. There couldn't be many of us, just a few. I don't know whether we can call it "collaboration" when we were trying to reduce, to however small a degree, the suffering of people who were about to die. For example, I would help the elderly people to get undressed and I tried to stop people being hit.

Once, I saw a mother with her two daughters; they must have been about twelve. They didn't get undressed; they just stood there, staring at the others, petrified. They came from Belgium, certainly from a well-off, elegant family. So they wouldn't be beaten, I spoke to them in French – or, at least, in pidgin French. "Madame," I told her, "hurry, because the German, he is coming, he will beat you, kill you." I realized that she was ashamed of getting undressed in public. So I told her, "Look, everybody isn't going to see you! Don't you worry yourself," and I stood in front of them, with my back turned to them, so they'd have a bit of privacy. Out of the corner of my eye, I saw they'd finally decided to get undressed. If the German had seen them, they'd certainly have been beaten. At least I made sure they were spared that. They went off with everybody else.

Did people try to ask you any questions?

No, not that I remember. They were completely dazed after their journey and focusing on what they had to do right now. Some just stood there, trying to understand what was going to happen. It took at least an hour or an hour and a half for them to get undressed. Sometimes as much as two hours. It depended on the people; the more elderly people there were, the longer it took. The first people who went into the gas chamber could be waiting there for more than an hour. Some women hurried in to get it over with more quickly. They thought the showers would be cleaner for the first in, but in the end, they suffered almost more than the others, as they waited there, naked.

Did things happen the same way when a group of prisoners selected inside the camp were sent to their deaths?

It was quite rare for those prisoners to be sent to our crematorium. Selections within the camp often took place on big Jewish holidays, especially Yom Kippur. When, in spite of everything, a group like that did arrive, it was worse than anything else. They already knew they were being sent to the gas chamber, to a certain death. Generally speaking, they had spent time in an isolated barrack, until the Germans thought there were enough of them to be sent to the gas chamber without wasting Zyklon B. The room was very big, and the more people who were crammed in, the less gas the Germans needed to kill their victims.

In general, those people were now so weak, sick, and resigned that they didn't make very much fuss. In the camp jargon, those prisoners, reduced as they were to the extreme limit of their strength, just skin and bones, were called *"Muselmänner"* (Muslims). I think the word comes from the position they would assume when they collapsed from exhaustion during the interminable roll calls; they did everything they could so as not to fall down, and summoned up the last of their strength to stay upright, but when they finally lost the last of their strength, their knees crumpled under the weight of their bodies, and their heads were so heavy they flopped forward. They ended up on the ground, in the position of Muslims at prayer. When the kapo didn't finish them off there and then, he noted their identity number for the next selection.

And what happened when these prisoners arrived in the Crematorium?

They had to get undressed without making much fuss. When there weren't too many of them, the Germans made them go directly through the service door that leads straight into the atrium. I remember that, on one occasion, a spontaneous little rebellion broke out among them. They refused to walk down the few steps and stayed in the entrance, blocking the way, so that nobody else could go down. But they didn't have time to do much. Moll wasn't far away, and he arrived just then, and started shouting. When he saw that wasn't enough, he picked up an enormous pestle that was generally used to grind the bones. With all his strength, he brought it crashing down on the heads of those standing nearest to him. He certainly cracked their skulls open, he was so powerful. The others were terrified, and had no choice but to go in, even if they knew perfectly well where they were going.

And did those who were too weak and who were sent to the Crematorium in trucks suffer the same fate?

The ones who arrived by truck were more often than not the ones who had been left behind in the train carriages. Whenever a train arrived, all of the people who couldn't walk any more, the sick, the handicapped, and the elderly, were loaded into the trucks and then unloaded in the Crematorium yard. But in general they tended to be sent to Crematoria IV or V, not very often to us in Crematorium III, nor II. When there wasn't enough room in those other crematoria, in that case alone they were sent to ours. There usually weren't more

"Naked women being unloaded," David Olère, 1946. Wash and China ink on paper. Ghetto Fighters Museum, Galilee, Israel

than about thirty of them. The trucks unloaded them onto a platform, like sand being poured out. The poor victims fell on top of one another. Those people who in normal times could hardly stand upright. . . . The pain of the fall and the humiliation must have been terrible. We had to help them get up and get undressed, and then take them inside the building, to a place where an SS man was waiting to execute them in cold blood, one by one.

For us, this was by far the most difficult task to accomplish. . . . There couldn't be anything harder than taking people to their deaths and holding them while they were executed. One time, I had to help an old woman get undressed. Like all elderly people, she clung to her things. And then, when faced with a man she didn't know, the poor woman was completely distraught. Every time I tried to take her stockings off, she pulled them back up again; I'd roll them down on one side, she'd pull them up on the other. But it was starting to get dangerous, since if the German waited too long, it might cost me my life. I didn't know what to do. . . . I started to get nervous. It's one of the things that's stayed in my mind, like . . . I was at the end of my tether; I grabbed hold of her forcibly to take off her stockings. I'd have torn them if necessary – anything to get them off her. The poor woman was protecting what she could. But she ended up the same as all the rest.

Where was the SS man, in cases such as that?

If you went up the three steps, you found yourself in the room with the ovens. You had to walk past them behind, on the side where the ashes were taken out. The German generally positioned himself at the far end, just hidden behind the corner of the last oven. We walked past him as if we were going to go up the stairs that led to the attic. The victims hardly saw him, and as soon as we'd passed him, he shot at point-blank range into the back of their necks. After a while, they changed their method and started using an air rifle, since a pistol bullet was too big and the impact was too close, and shattered the victim's skull. This was particularly unpleasant for the German, who got spattered by the blood. The person accompanying the victim needed to know the technique: he had to hold the victims by the ear, at arm's length, then the German shot, and, before the person fell to the ground, we had to take great care to make them lower their heads, since otherwise the blood spurted out like a fountain. If by accident a little blood fell on the SS man, he took it out on us and didn't hesitate to punish us or even kill us there and then. This almost happened with my brother. At that time he was already with me in Crematorium III. He wasn't able to lower the victim's head quickly enough and the blood spurted out onto the German. As luck would have it, I wasn't far away and I intervened, saying in German, "*Das ist mein Bruder!*" "That's my brother!" That could have created problems for me, too, but instead the

German calmed down and let us leave. From that time on, my brother always avoided as much as possible this particularly horrible task. For me, the hardest thing was having to let the dead person drop. Feeling the person's weight, in that fall in which I could not help but participate. It made me ill, hearing the body slump to the ground, even if I knew the person was already dead, and I did everything I could to soften the fall.

You see, the men in the Sonderkommando were also forced to do that kind of thing. It can't be denied, nor can it be said that it didn't exist or isn't true. And yet, in this case, I acknowledge that I feel a bit complicit, even if I didn't kill them. We had no choice, no other possibility in that hell! If I'd refused to do so, the German would have jumped on me and killed me immediately, to make an example of me. Fortunately, these groups weren't sent to our Crematorium very often. Two or three times at most.

The men of the Sonderkommando told me how things happened in Crematorium V. It seems that, over there, the trucks unloaded the living victims into the ditches that were burning under the open sky. I didn't see this personally, so I can't confirm it, but it seems perfectly possible to me that they didn't even bother to kill people before throwing them into the fire. With us, it took longer, since the German had to kill them one by one.

Did you go to Crematoria IV and V, and were you personally able to note the differences with Crematoria II and III?

Yes, I went there four or five times, to see my brother who worked there for the first few months. Later on, I managed to get him brought over to my crematorium, since the work was better organized there, so a little less demanding. In particular, in our crematorium there were no open graves, as the bodies were burned in the ovens. But over there, the ovens often failed to work or were inadequate, so the bodies had to be burned in open ditches. When they needed extra hands, they asked my kapo, Lemke,[5] to go over with a few people to help. I went over several times, but it was always an excuse to see my brother.

I remember that on the road, as we came back from Crematorium IV, the German would occasionally ask my cousin Yakob Gabbai to sing. "*Greco! Singen!*" he told him. Yakob had a fine baritone voice and he then started singing Greek patriotic songs that the Germans couldn't understand. Throughout the camp you heard a song, "*Tin Elliniki simea* . . .," the words of which meant "The Greek flag, my God how I love it, my mother, I will never abandon my native land to foreigners, I would rather die." It was as if the Greeks had suddenly and victoriously entered the camp.

I didn't go into Crematoria IV and V, so I can only say what I saw from the outside. I'm often amazed when I think back – I was so curious, how can it be that I never tried to get in to see what was inside? If I'd thought for a second that I was going to survive, I'd have noted everything so that I could relate it. . . . But anyway, I saw only the ditches. These were like big swimming pools; the bodies were brought up and then placed in them by Sonderkommando men who knew how to do their job. If I remember correctly, there were two ditches in front of the entrance, on the Crematorium side. I know that historians say there were more ditches, but when I was there, I saw only two working. They resembled the ditches that I saw near Bunker 2, with one difference: in Crematorium V, the ditches supplemented the ovens.[6]

---

[5] Lemke (Chaim) Pliszko, born in 1918 in Czerwony Bor, was deported on January 16, 1943 from the Łomża transit camp.
[6] By late spring 1944, five cremation ditches in the open were used within the area of Crematorium V. Three were in the space that faced the entrance of the biggest gas chamber and two on the side of the Crematorium, between the building and the barbed wire.

Crematoria IV and V were smaller than Crematoria II and III; the ovens did not work as well, and were less powerful. The ditches made it possible for the corpses to be eliminated more quickly, as it takes a long time to burn seven hundred bodies in such small ovens. Especially when the ovens didn't work properly. In our crematoria, there could be as many as one thousand, eight hundred people.

On average, the whole process in which a single convoy was eliminated was supposed to last seventy-two hours. Killing them was quick; the thing that took such a long time was burning the corpses. That was actually the Germans' main problem: getting rid of the bodies. The ditches made it possible to go a bit faster.

When you went to Crematoria IV and V, were you obliged to help as well?

In principle, yes, I should have helped out. The kapos could order us, for example, to carry the corpses from one place to a ditch. But the ones giving orders over there weren't those of my crematorium. So we weren't running too many risks if we were a bit obstructive – for instance, we could do things slowly and not in the correct way. We weren't the regular workers, just helpers, supernumeraries. We didn't need to worry about not doing things on time, nor about being blamed if things went wrong.

I remember a terrible episode that I witnessed while I was there. Moll, the dreaded *Malahamoves*, flew into a rage against two young Greek brothers, Alberto and Raul Jachon. He ordered them to bring a basin into which he poured some flammable liquid. Then that cursed Moll ordered them to take off their shoes and place their feet into the basin. He tossed in a match and the mixture quickly caught fire. Obviously, they jumped out of the basin to stop themselves getting burned, and this drove Moll furious with rage. He wanted to "amuse" himself a little more, so he ordered them to climb the barbed-wire fence, and duped them into thinking that if they reached the other side, they'd be free. Just then, there wasn't any current in the barbed wire. They managed to climb quite high. But, of course, Moll had no intention of keeping his promise; he shot them down like dogs.

So did your brother work in that crematorium?

Yes, but actually, I saw him only once in Crematorium IV. Although I went there on several occasions, just to find out how he was, I didn't find him. When I finally did see him, I already knew that it was more terrible and demanding to work in his crematorium than in mine. At least we didn't have to transport the bodies to the ditches. Even more than wanting to be with him, I wanted to make sure that he wouldn't stay in that place. So I did everything to bring him across. In any case, I wanted us to be able to spend our last moments together. I was convinced that, after the third month, there'd be a selection and the men in the Sonderkommando would be eliminated. I wasn't expecting to live beyond those three months, so, when I saw that the end was approaching, I went to see the kapo of my crematorium, Lemke. He was a Polish Jew, not a bad man – we respected him. The kapos in the crematoria were not like the other kapos in the camp. They were all Jews and they didn't beat the prisoners, they didn't use any sadistic violence on us and, in general, they were the ones who, together with a few others, organized the October revolt.

Lemke was a somewhat reserved man; he didn't say much and he wasn't easy to get on with. He merely said to us, "*Hevre!*" "[To work,] brothers!" The only risk you ran if you didn't obey him was that he might designate you for the next selection. But I managed to establish a relationship with him;

I wouldn't say one of friendship, but one of trust. This made it possible for me to go to him and ask him, in my own way, in my rudimentary German, whether it would be possible to transfer my brother. He asked me whether my brother was someone strong and of good character. I answered yes; he was very muscular, physically he was even stronger than I – and I also told him how we often played duets together: I played the harmonica while he danced. At that time I didn't really understand why he'd asked me those questions. But the important thing was that he accepted. Later, I realized he was already thinking of the revolt and wanted to have with him men who were both physically strong and strong of character.

   To bring my brother over from Crematorium IV to Crematorium III, we had to exchange a *Stück*, in other words a "piece," since we were considered to be nothing more than pieces. Lemke came to an agreement with the kapo of Crematorium IV. One day, when four men from our crematorium had gone off with a pot to get the soup from *Lager d*, one of them, quite an elderly Greek, took the place of my brother, who came over at the same time from Crematorium IV. This was how he joined me in Crematorium III. For the Germans and the kapos, it was all the same, one "piece" here or there . . . the important thing was for the numbers to be right. They didn't even look at the identity numbers; we were merely *Stücke*.

You say that the kapos in the Sonderkommando didn't use violence. What about the SS men in the Crematorium?

There weren't many SS in the Crematorium. Generally speaking, there were two SS men assigned to each crematorium: one on daytime duty, the other at night. There were more of them when a convoy arrived, but there were only two permanent guards. Most of the time, they stayed put in their little corner and didn't come out until the convoys arrived, and from time to time to keep an eye on us. But in principle they didn't need to come and check very often, since that was the kapos' job. If everything wasn't finished in three days, it meant that we hadn't worked hard enough. But the kapo generally stepped in first.

The Sonderkommando was a particular case. Overall, the SS who oversaw us left us alone. They didn't fly off the handle with us, since our work was too important in their eyes and they didn't try to undermine us. Apart from Moll, of course, who was in charge of all the crematoria. That cursed "Angel of Death" was the worst of all. The minute he arrived in a crematorium it was the end of the world, and even the German guard was afraid that he might be blamed for everything and anything. Moll used every pretext to yell, terrorize, and punish. There were other cases: in my crematorium, I remember one of the guards who was a veritable brute. He was very tall, had a big face, but I can't remember his name. He resembled one of the SS men drawn by David Olère. This man enjoyed personally killing his victims.[7]

In actual fact, killing the victims with a revolver shot was never a problem for any of the Germans, apart from a single SS man I knew. He wasn't even German, actually, he was Dutch, and I always found him more humane than the others. I spoke with him once, and he told me he'd volunteered for the SS, since he believed in the rigor and efficiency of the Germans. When he realized what things were really like, it was already too late for him. He had to stay put and keep his mouth shut, otherwise he risked being sent to the Russian front or being eliminated immediately. But he avoided as much as possible having to kill people himself. When he

---

[7] This was probably SS-Unterscharführer Johann Gorges, who worked in Auschwitz between spring 1941 and January 1945. He died a free man in his home town, Trier, on July 18, 1971.

"Portrait of SS man Georges, one of the cruelest torturers in the camp,"
David Olère, 1947. Wash and China ink on paper. Private collection

found himself in these situations, he preferred to call over
another SS man so he wouldn't have to kill anyone himself. To
avoid the other Germans finding out about his hesitations, he
had to pretend and to give the impression that he was as harsh
as they were. So, to give that impression, he often hit the prisoners; he'd worked out an entire system to avoid hurting his
victims. He used a cane of bamboo, split in the middle. When
he hit someone, the pain was minimal, but the noise made by
the two tips as they came together made it sound like a whip
being loudly cracked. He was the only SS man I ever knew to
behave like that. The others were all vicious animals, without
humanity. When it was necessary to kill, they killed without
compunction. They created a huge chaos to frighten people

and disorientate them as soon as they arrived. The broken families, the children terrorized and beaten – nobody knew how to react other than by keeping in line, and this was how they managed to do what they wanted with us.

The Dutchman was more humane; I even had a conversation with him when he happened to come into the chimney room where I was alone. I'd picked up, among the clothes left there, a very fine harmonica, a Höhner. I knew how to play it, as a matter of fact, since I'd been lucky enough to have one when I was a child. From time to time, when I could take a breather and let the others carry on without me for a minute, I'd go into that square room and take out my harmonica for a bit of relaxation, or I simply leaned against the window ledge to get some fresh air. This room was, so to speak, my refuge. It was small, with a window and, in the middle, the huge, square brick conduit of the chimney that ran across the room. One day when I was there, quietly playing my harmonica, the door opened and suddenly revealed this Dutch SS man. I immediately stood up and took off my cap. He came into the room and with an encouraging wave of his hand he told me, "*Spiel!*" "Play!" I hesitated for a moment, but he insisted. So I played the first tune that came into my head. He really liked it and said he wanted to learn how to play too. I couldn't read music, and told him that I played only by ear. So he motioned me to hand him the instrument so he could try in turn. The most surprising thing was that he took the harmonica and placed it to his lips without first wiping it, as everyone naturally does. He tried to play, but only inaudible sounds emerged. He gave it back to me with a shrug, and we started to talk.

Did he never have to lead selections inside the Sonderkommando?

No, he was only a guard. And it so happens that, when I joined the Sonderkommando, the work was of a kind that my group never had to undergo any selection. Quite the opposite – they never stopped adding to the number of persons who worked in the crematoria. It was the old hands who told us how the selections were carried out. It wasn't like in the other parts of the camp. With us, the German went to see the kapo and told him how many people had to be "transferred." We knew that "transferred" meant "eliminated." The kapo decided whom to send, and in general he chose the latest arrivals. I also have to say that the Polish Jews tended to help each other, whereas we Sephardim were generally less secure. That's why I tried to gain the confidence of my kapo, Lemke.

We were always expecting a selection to take place, which would mean it was all over. For example, when they sent us to the *Sauna* for a shower. This wasn't so much for disinfection purposes, since in the Sonderkommando we could change clothes quite regularly so as to avoid the risks of an epidemic being caused by lice. But their aim was to get us used to these "excursions" in small groups. So, if they'd wanted to eliminate us, it would have been easier for them to pretend they were taking us to the *Sauna*.

And when you did go to the Sauna, you didn't wonder whether this was the last time?

No, we didn't think anything. On the contrary, it was even a liberation for us. Some people asked me if it wouldn't be better to get it over with. Perhaps – or even certainly. But I didn't think of it; we had to keep on going, day by day, without asking ourselves any questions: keep on living, even if it was terrible. To my knowledge, nobody in the Sonderkommando committed suicide. I know that some of them said they wanted to live at any price. Personally, I think I'd rather have died. But each time, some words of my mother's used to come to my mind: "While there's life, there's hope." We were too close to death, but we carried on, day by day. I think we needed a special strength to get through it all, a psychological and physical strength.

Still, one man in the Sonderkommando was very thin and certainly ill. I think he was a Polish intellectual, someone respected, since everyone left him alone. Lemke protected him and the guards didn't say anything. I never saw him working. He didn't even need to come down to roll call. Until the day when Moll arrived and demanded that everyone come down. For him, it was the end. But it's a long story and I need to go back to the beginning.

It all happened a short time after my arrival in the Sonderkommando. Some camp prisoners were still working on the extension of the railway. Those right at the end of the ramp, in other words near the Crematorium, were Jews from Rhodes; they spoke Ladino, as we did. They'd heard that there were Greeks working in the Crematorium and that our group didn't lack anything. The German allowed them to sing as they worked, so they made up a tune and asked us, in Ladino, to send them some food and clothes. After some hesitation, we finally prepared a little parcel with a loaf wrapped up in shirts, and threw it over the barbed wire to them. The first parcel got across and the German guard watching the prisoners let them take it. But just as we were throwing the second, Moll's motorbike appeared. He got off in the Crematorium, demanding to know who had thrown the parcel. As he didn't have time to sort it out there and then, he promised he'd come back the next day to punish the guilty men.

And back he came the following morning. We were immediately ordered to assemble in front of the Crematorium, but there were two people missing from roll call: the man I'm calling "the intellectual" and . . . I. As chance would have it, that morning I was outside the building, in the distant corner where the ashes were ground up. Far from the others,

absorbed in my own thoughts, I didn't hear the kapos ordering everyone to assemble. A kapo found me and ordered me to
get a move on. I started to run the minute I heard *Malahamoves*
shouting. I was terror-stricken at the idea of what he was going
to do to me. I couldn't stop thinking of that man he'd killed in
front of me, in Bunker 2. I had the end of a cigarette dangling
from my lips and the *Mütze* (beret) that we had to take off in
front of the Germans. I ran and saw Moll only at the last
second, turning onto the square where the roll call was held.
I spat out the cigarette, but almost forgot to remove my cap.
Of course, he started yelling. Then he pushed me, and stuck
out his leg so that I'd trip over it. You had to get to your feet
right away, otherwise the punishment was even harsher. He
hit me a second time; I fell over and got up again. Then he
told me to line up with the others. I was convinced he was
going to take advantage of this to shoot me in the back. I don't
know if I flew or ran, but in any case I got to my place in record
time.

The man who had thrown the parcels confessed. Everybody
knew that, if no one said anything, the punishment would be
collective and just as painful. He was punished with twenty-
five lashes of the whip. In the sadistic system of the Germans,
it was one of the deportees who had to administer the whip-
ping to his comrade's back. The Germans checked that the
lashes were strong enough, and if they weren't, both men were
punished. I can say that I was lucky: I was given just two lashes,
so I got off lightly.

As for the "intellectual," he was obliged to come down, in
spite of the kapo's explanations. I'd never really seen him
before. He was pale, skinny, and sickly. In my opinion he must
have been over forty-five. Before he came down, he managed
to hide a blanket under his clothes and thus appear less skinny
than he really was. Moll was furious at having been kept waiting and flew into a rage at him, ordering him to be whipped.

He chose a Russian for the task, showing him how hard he needed to hit the man. To begin with, protected by the blanket, he didn't suffer too much under the sting of the lashes. But instead of pretending to be in pain, he just stood there. Moll was sufficiently used to this kind of punishment to know how prisoners were supposed to react. He wasn't taken in for long and ordered the prisoner to take his trousers down. When he saw the blanket, his anger intensified and he literally beat the poor man to death.

Did any members of the Sonderkommando try to escape?

To my knowledge, this happened only once during my time in the Sonderkommando. I know that, outside the Sonderkommando, it happened several times and some men managed to escape.[8] But when they told their stories, nobody believed them. The governments, Churchill and the rest, weren't bothered about the Jews; they simply wanted to win the war. If they'd wanted to save the Jews, they could have done so earlier. In any case, as far as the men from my Crematorium who tried to escape are concerned, I know that it wasn't planned. They tried to do so when the opportunity presented itself.

It was two Greeks who made the attempt: Hugo Venezia (the son of the Baruch I've already mentioned) and Alex Errera. Nobody ever remembers their story, but Errera, Alekos as the Greeks called him, was a real hero. Before being deported, he'd been a captain in the Greek navy and he was greatly respected by us. One day, the Germans ordered these two to accompany the truck that had come to fetch the ashes, so as to throw them into the river Soła. The two men had to scatter the ashes in the water by placing a cistern on the

---

[8] Several members attempted to escape from the Sonderkommando.

ground and gathering up the last ashes with a spade to make sure that absolutely no trace remained.

That day I knew that something had happened when the alarm was sounded. In the camp, there usually were several types of siren signals, but the one that sounded continuously meant the situation was serious. For the Germans, the escape of a member of the Sonderkommando was really serious; they absolutely couldn't allow a man who had seen the inside of the gas chambers to get away. They immediately increased the number of guards around the Crematorium and ordered interminable roll calls throughout the camp. I found out that, for some people, these roll calls had lasted all night, but not for us; the Germans didn't want our work to be interrupted for too long.

We found out what had happened when Hugo Venezia returned. He told us that the SS man accompanying them had gotten in next to the driver and they'd stayed in the rear with the load of ashes. Before they reached the river, Errera had devised a plan and told Hugo what he'd need to do. Errera was to knock down the guard who'd come to open the door for them, while Hugo would go and take the driver by surprise, before jumping into the river. When the truck stopped, they waited for the SS man to come around and tell them to get out; while he was opening up, Errera knocked him out with a great blow of his spade. When he heard the noise, the driver, who was reading a paper, looked through his rear-view mirror and came out of the truck with his pistol in his hand. Hugo Venezia told us he'd been unable to do anything; he stood there paralyzed, frozen stiff with fear when faced with the driver pointing his pistol. He was a young man of barely eighteen, whereas Errera had experience and certainly greater strength of character too. Without waiting, he immediately jumped into the river and started swimming to the other shore. The driver shot at him, but the regulation revolver's range couldn't reach him. So, seizing the guard's rifle that was lying on the ground, the German started firing off those "dum-dum" bullets that are designed to fragment inside the body and cause the maximum amount of damage. Errera was hit in the thigh, but he continued until he had reached the other bank. The alarm was raised, and the manhunt that was immediately organized lasted all night and the following day. But the wound must have been grave; Errera must have lost a lot of blood and he did not survive his escape. His body was found and brought back to Crematorium II. In the meantime, Hugo, brought back by the driver, told us everything he'd seen. The very next day, the Germans came for him and he was never seen again. As for Errera, he was brought back for an autopsy. Then his body, totally dismembered and disfigured, was exhibited on a table in the yard of the Crematorium. They obliged all of us to pass in front of the table to look at the deformed and unrecognizable face of our old companion. The Germans were extremely agitated, and anyone who looked away was beaten with a stick. Then we carried him into the room where the ovens stood and recited a *kaddish* before burning his body. Nobody ever talks about this episode, since nobody has really carried out a study on the fate of the Greeks at Birkenau.

4

SONDERKOMMANDO: THE WORK CONTINUES

From the moment we started working in the Crematorium, the Germans made us sleep there. There was a place set up for us, under the roof, above the room with the furnaces. The roof had a mansard, but it was quite high; as far as the bed, you could stand completely upright. Everyone had his own bed, unlike in the other barracks in the camp where the prisoners had to squeeze together in groups of five on filthy bunks. The two rows of beds were separated by a set of shelves extending the full length of the room. These shelves contained over two hundred urns all lined up, and all identical. I wanted to know what was in the urns, so I took one and opened it up. It was filled with a very fine ash and had a little medallion on it, bearing a number. It must have been the identity number of a prisoner. I later discovered that the Germans kept these urns for the prisoners' families. This was certainly not done for the Jews, but for the Christians who'd died in the camp, from starvation, illness, or whatever. The Germans informed the family that the prisoner had died of an illness and that it was possible to collect the ashes in exchange for a payment of two hundred marks. In fact, in each of those urns were the mixed ashes of several people and the urns may not have contained a single trace of the person designated.

Do you remember any other members of the Sonderkommando who were with you? Did you see any French Jews, for example?

I remember a few people, especially the Greeks who were with me. But the majority of members of the Sonderkommando were Poles. Some also came from other countries in Eastern Europe, but all of them could speak Yiddish, except for us, the Greeks, who spoke Ladino among ourselves.

   I didn't see any Frenchmen, otherwise I'd have spoken with them. David Olère, for instance – I didn't know that he'd been deported from France; as far as I was concerned, he was a Pole who spoke Yiddish. I never heard him speak French, but in any case, as I've said before, we didn't often speak together. Most of the time I didn't even know the others' names. If we needed anything, we just said *"Du!"* "You!" I spoke a bit of German, but certain Greeks, who didn't speak Yiddish, didn't even know a word of German. In general, we signed to each other with our hands, or our feet . . . whatever way we could.

Were there any non-Jews with you?

No, all the men working in the Sonderkommando were Jews. The only exceptions, as far as I'm aware, were a few Soviet prisoners of war sent to our crematorium. But they didn't work there, or at least, I never saw them working. They merely recovered what they could from the victims' clothes. In Crematorium II, there was also a non-Jewish German prisoner. His name was Karol, and he was a common law criminal prisoner. Everyone was convinced that he'd been sent there to act as a spy for the Germans. He was always elegant but he behaved like a pig. The men tried to avoid him as much as possible. I'll have occasion to say more about him when we come to speak about the Sonderkommando revolt.

As for the few Russians I've just mentioned, they'd initially been interned in the camp at Auschwitz I. But when there were too many of them together there they were forever organizing escape plans. So, in order to avoid this, the Germans separated them out into different sectors of the camp. In my crematorium, there must have been six or eight of them, all soldiers. I remember two of them in particular, one called Misha and the other called Ivan. If my memory serves me right, there was a third called Sasha. Ivan was the youngest; he had a child's chubby face. We communicated with our hands and feet, and I found out that they'd been taken prisoner when they tried to parachute down behind the front line.

In the Crematorium, I never saw them work. The kapo didn't ask anything of them and left them alone, since, unlike us Jews, they weren't there to work. There was considerable animosity between the Russians and the Poles, especially the Polish Jews. But they didn't have any problems with us Jews from Greece. All they ever did was drink vodka, eat sausages, and smoke cigarettes. One day, one of the Russians invited me to share his feast. He said to me, "*Grecki, idi cyuda!*" "Greek guy, come here!" I hesitated to go over, since I hadn't understood and was sure he'd insulted me, as the Russians habitually insulted everyone. When I went over, he offered me a glass of vodka. It was the first time I'd had any; I took a sip, but they forced me to knock it back in one gulp. I almost choked to death. A Russian handed me a hunk of bread and told me to breathe out hard into it. That's how the burning sensation went away.

They had no difficulty in getting as much vodka and food as they wanted. When the groups arrived and finished undressing, the Russians joined the prisoners whose job it was to bundle the clothes together (as we'd done on the first day in the Crematorium). But instead of really making bundles to send to the Kanada, they had just one aim: to rummage round in the clothes to find any valuables hidden among them. Everyone did this: some were simply trying to find something to eat, others were after valuables. In this way we could salvage various things and not suffer too much from hunger. We also took advantage of the situation to change our clothes when they got too ragged. We just had to throw the old ones onto the pile of clothes to be sent to the Kanada and then to help ourselves, discreetly, from the heap left by the victims. We had to make sure that we weren't caught in the act, but usually it was easy. The Russians did nothing else. And then they had their system for exchanging these objects for vodka or food from outside the camp. Those things came into the camp thanks to the Polish *Vorarbeiter* (foremen) from the town of Oświęcim. The Poles were taking a risk, but they profited from the exchange. For example, an old newspaper could be exchanged for a gold ring. In general, these highly risky exchanges passed through several hands and took place discreetly when it was time for the men to get their soup. The kapo would send four men to fetch the soup (even through two were enough) because this was the only time when the men in the Sonderkommando could have any contact with other prisoners and thus with the outside world. But it wasn't easy, since, in order to avoid this happening, the Germans always made the Sonderkommando go first. In those cases, we never had to wait. But in spite of everything, they managed to establish contact.

So there could, in spite of everything, be relations between the men in the Sonderkommando and other prisoners?

Yes, the men who were designated by the kapo to go and fetch the soup managed to establish these contacts. In fact, that's partially what made it possible to organize the revolt. The women's camp was another venue. For this, one had to bribe the German guard so that he'd agree to take prisoners into the women's camp and turn a blind eye. Lemke would sometimes organize little feasts by exchanging the jewels that were given to him when they were found [in the clothes left by those who were gassed], so he could invite the German guards and ensure they'd be indulgent. But obviously, going into the women's camp wasn't simply done for the purpose of organizing the revolt. Even if it didn't happen often, I suppose some went to see their girlfriends. And once they were in, if they did do anything with the women, I don't know, I wasn't there, so I can't say.

Did they do so, in your view?

Yes, I think some of them did. Frankly, I myself couldn't have done so. I don't even know how they could have felt any desire. After the Liberation, I heard some absurd rumors about what was supposed to have happened in the Sonderkommando with dead women. But these are just lies, sick rumors initiated by people trying to undermine and discredit the men working in the Sonderkommando. I never heard anything like that during the eight months I spent there.

On the other hand, I do remember that, one day, among the corpses brought out of the gas chamber, the men found the body of an incredibly beautiful woman. She had the perfect beauty of ancient statues. Those who were supposed to put her into the oven couldn't bring themselves to destroy such a pure image. They kept her body with them for as long as they could, then they were obliged to burn her as well as the others. I think that was the only time I really "looked." Otherwise, everything happened mechanically; there was nothing to see. Even in the room where people got undressed, you didn't pay any attention; you had no right to feel moved.

Sometimes, in spite of everything, we were touched, and affected, like the day I saw that woman and her son arrive; they'd tried to hide in the Crematorium yard. . . . They were part of a convoy from Łódź. There must have been one thousand, seven hundred people sent to our crematorium from this transport. Everything proceeded as usual. The people entered the gas chamber, the German threw in the gas, then our macabre task began. We worked normally all day long, then the night team took over. The next morning, at around eight or nine, one of the men came in surprise to tell us that a woman with a small boy of about twelve were in the Crematorium yard. Nobody knew how they'd managed to get there, but when we looked at them more closely, it became clear that they were part of the group that had been sent to their death the day before. We stared at each other in astonishment. Then I went over to her to try to find out more. I don't know if she'd climbed up the fence or if she'd passed between the tree trunks and the barbed-wire fence. I really don't know how she'd done it, since everything was closed off, and she must have climbed over. The fact remains that she'd stayed hidden with her son. The tall grass – it was a summer month – enabled them to hide from the guards. But they then came face to face with the barbed wire, and no way of getting out. When the mother realized there was no exit, she headed in the direction of the Crematorium, hoping to escape that way. She couldn't stop crying and saying over and over that, for a long time, she had worked in the ghetto as a seamstress for the German soldiers and she could still be useful.

The German on guard realized there was a problem and came into the yard to see what was happening. The woman started to implore him, repeating the same things she had told us. To calm her down, the German told her, "You're right, Madam, we'll see what we can do, follow me." But everyone knew: he was going to kill them as soon as they were inside. I don't remember whether he told them to get undressed and start off by going into disinfection, but he didn't waste much time and killed them both with a bullet in the back of the neck. Subsequently, the Germans had the tall grass between the fence and the barbed wire cut, so as to avoid that type of "incident."

Do you think that that woman, coming as she did from the last ghetto in Poland, knew where she had been sent?

I don't know what exactly she did know, but it's true that the deportees who'd been in the ghettos knew much more than the others. They had lost any illusions, they were exhausted, psychologically at the end of their tether after all those years in the ghetto. When they arrived, they allowed themselves to be guided to the "disinfection" room, without really understanding, or trying to understand, what was happening.

One certain thing is that there were very marked differences between those who came from the ghettos and the others. Those who came from Holland or Hungary, for instance, still had a few valuables on them, and were still relatively strong, while the deportees from the ghettos had nothing but lice. You could see that most of them had lost even the will to live. There weren't many who still had any strength and hope. Seeing them so resigned, I often wondered whether we, too (who also had become docile), could have done something; refused to obey orders. But there was no choice: those who did refuse were killed before the others with a bullet through the back of the neck, end of story.

Did you see anyone refusing to join the Sonderkommando?

Yes. One day, three young religious Jews from Hungary were put to one side so they could join the Sonderkommando. They were still wearing their kaftans, their hats, their long locks. They refused to accept the Germans' orders. I didn't see them go in, but I know they were made to get undressed and that they went up the three steps, like those who were executed with a revolver shot. That's how they died. I suppose that others were immediately taken to replace them. There wasn't exactly a shortage.

Were there any religious men among you?

Some people prayed every day. I know that in other parts of the camp it was impossible or much too dangerous, but we didn't run too many risks as the Germans never came up to where the men of the Sonderkommando slept. You could easily pick up prayer books, even though the men in question didn't need them – they knew the prayers by heart.

I'd never been religious – not even a believer. I always found that respecting the Ten Commandments was enough for me. In Birkenau, I never asked myself this question; since I wasn't religious, I left God out of all that. But I couldn't understand why they continued to call on him: "*Adonai, Adonai*" ("Lord, Lord"). . . . What were they thinking? That Adonai was going to save them? What an idea! We were all living beings in the process of crossing the frontier into death.

People often talk of the solidarity that existed between detainees. What was your experience of this?

There was solidarity only when you had enough for yourself; otherwise, you had to be selfish if you were going to survive.

In the Crematorium, you could indulge in solidarity, since we each had enough to survive. I'm not talking about helping a friend and taking over from him to give him a chance to recuperate. I'm talking about having enough to eat. For those who didn't have enough to eat, solidarity was no longer an option. So even when you had to take something from someone in order to survive, many people did so. We had enough to eat and were in a position to try to get food to others, even if this involved taking a few risks. For example, during the week, the men who went to fetch the soup for the Sonderkommando often left it on the way back for the prisoners working on extending the rail tracks. We left our pot, which was full, and took theirs, which was already empty. We didn't go short, since everyone in the Sonderkommando had enough bread and canned food. Even if the deportees arrived in the Crematorium without their suitcases and not much in their pockets, there were so many of them that we still could find something to put aside. Elsewhere, this wasn't possible. Showing solidarity was a luxury that few could afford; a mouthful of food given to someone else was a mouthful less for you. . . .

What did the other prisoners in the camp think of the Sonderkommando members?

I didn't have any contact with the other prisoners in the camp, so I don't really know. I never went to fetch the soup and I was never in the women's camp. The question didn't arise when we were in the camp. On the other hand, I did find out later that some people were jealous of the fact we sometimes got extra. Others held us partly responsible for what happened in the Crematorium. But that's completely wrong: only the Germans killed. We were forced, whereas collaborators, in general, are volunteers. It's important to write that we had no choice. Those who refused were immediately killed with a bullet through the back of the neck. For the Germans, it was no big deal; if they killed ten, another fifty arrived. For us, we had to survive, get enough to eat . . . there was no other possibility. Not for anybody. And then, we could no longer reason with our brains and think about what was happening . . . we'd become robots.

These days I often ask myself: what would I have done if they'd forced me to kill in person? What would I have done? I don't know. Would I have refused, knowing full well that they'd have killed me on the spot?

Did you ever ask yourself that question while you were in the camp?

No, not in the camp, never. There, you didn't even have the possibility of asking yourself those questions. It was only after the Liberation that those questions came to haunt me. We had to help the elderly people get undressed, but what if we'd been ordered to kill them? The Germans were capable of every perversion to humiliate us. For example, just for fun, a German would order a father to whip his son. If the father refused, it was the other way round: he ordered the son to strike his father. The father himself told his son to obey, and if both of them refused, they were both whipped, often to death. That was how things were – it was sadistic. You had to be lucky to avoid that kind of situation. And when you couldn't avoid them, then you were faced with terrible decisions; you had no control over anything.

Your only choice was to get used to it. Very quickly, too. On the first days, I wasn't even able to swallow my bread when I thought of all those corpses my hands had touched. But what could you do? A person had to eat. . . . After a week or two, you got used to it. You got used to everything. The same way that I'd gotten used to the sickening smell. After a while, you stopped registering it. You'd gotten onto a treadmill. But you didn't even realize, since, quite simply, you stopped thinking! During the first two or three weeks, I was constantly stunned by the enormity of the crime, but then you stop thinking. The first day, I was unable to close my eyes all night. I kept thinking of this terrible situation, of the way I'd allowed myself to be caught and brought to such a place. Even these days, the same questions continue to haunt me.

Unlike me, my brother has never wanted to recount his experience to schoolchildren. He often says to me: "Think about it – I myself often imagine that it was all just a bad dream, that it couldn't have existed. So put yourself in the place of others who are hearing this story now!" But I think it's precisely for this reason – because it is so completely unimaginable – that those people who can tell their story must do so. Those of us in the Sonderkommando may have had better conditions of day-to-day survival; we weren't as cold, we had more to eat, suffered less violence – but we had seen the worst, we were in it all day long, at the heart of hell.

And what if you'd been able to swap places with someone else in the camp?

Immediately – like a shot! Even though I realized that, in that instance, I might not have enough to eat. I'd have done it immediately, without hesitating for a second, at the risk of suffering a slow death. And yet I know how terrible it is to be hungry and the appalling pain it involves, but never mind. Even during the "death march" and later, in the camps to which I was evacuated and where I suffered like the other prisoners, I felt relieved that I'd left the Crematorium.

Did you never seriously think of escaping?

No, it was impossible, especially for a member of the Sonderkommando. Everyone was recaptured – and where would I have gone? I didn't speak Polish, and the risk of being denounced by the peasants was too high. The only ones who did try to escape, while I was in Birkenau, did it without planning, when an exceptional opportunity presented itself. I'm talking about Errera, of course, but he was recaptured and killed.

Did you ever talk or think about the future?

No, my horizons were restricted to the moment when I would be killed. Some people say they resisted because they still hoped to get free one day. But I didn't think I'd ever be able to free myself from that hell. I don't think any of the men in the Sonderkommando maintained such a naïve hope. There was no way of getting out. Except by miracle. . . . But nobody believed in miracles any more. We just carried on, day after day, knowing that the end was approaching.

Sometimes, in spite of everything, a slender hope would filter through, such as when we learned about the assassination attempt on Hitler. The Germans were beside themselves with rage that day, but for us it vaguely awakened a glimmer of light. Or when we learned that a member of our family was still alive. As on the day when I saw, or thought I saw, my sister. . . .

That day, I happened to be in Crematorium II. I sometimes happened to go there, when it wasn't my turn to work, to meet my friends from Greece. Crematorium II looked out on the women's camp. That day, I was leaning against the window, absorbed in my thoughts, when I thought I glimpsed my sister facing me, in front of the barbed-wire fence around the women's camp. In hindsight, I don't know if I did recognize her or just wanted to recognize her. I'd accepted the idea that I'd never see my mother and my two younger sisters again. But I still hoped that my older sister Rachel had been sent to work. I often thought of her, as I was doing on that day, as I gazed through the window at the women's camp. It was the end of the day, the sun had given way to a gray light, the typical Birkenau mist had hidden the shapes of things, when all of a sudden I caught sight of that shape. I was too far away to make her out clearly, but I thought I recognized my sister. I called, "Rachel!!" The echo carried my voice and she replied in Ladino, "Yes! Who are you?"

"Shlomo!"

"Shlomo! How are you? How very nice to hear your voice!"

We couldn't talk much, so I told her to come back to the same place at the same time the next day, and I'd have a parcel for her. And indeed, the next day, at the same time, the same figure came up. I'd prepared a bundle to throw over to her, with things to eat and objects that might be of use to her in the camp. Once again, we agreed to meet up the following day. And so on, over the next five or six days. But one evening she did not come, and I thought she must have been transferred or, worse, selected.

When I finally did see my sister, twelve years after the Liberation, she was living with her husband Aaron, in Israel. I went to see her in Haifa. In the taxi taking us to her house, I started to cry. In twelve years, since my deportation, I'd never cried . . . apart from once, when I cried with rage. But all of a sudden, my emotion at seeing my sister again had made all the poison I'd been building up inside myself all those years pour out. And I couldn't stop talking and weeping. Meanwhile my sister said nothing. I had kept all that pain inside myself . . . my mother . . . everything I'd seen! When I finally got a bit of a grip on myself, I reminded her of the business with the parcels

I'd thrown across. She didn't know what I was talking about. She told me she hadn't stayed in the women's camp at Birkenau. And there I'd been, taking so many risks on behalf of a woman I didn't know and who had pretended to be Rachel! I'd noticed that her voice was a bit different, but everything was different in that place . . . and then, I couldn't make her out clearly, I just saw a shape. Still, I'm happy I was able to help that woman; she certainly needed it just as much as my sister.

Did any member of the Sonderkommando around you ever recognize anyone from his own family in the gas chamber?

Yes, it happened to me. . . . It happened shortly before the Sonderkommando uprising, during the last gassings in the Crematorium. I happened to be in the undressing room, when a group of prisoners selected from the camp hospital arrived. There must have been two hundred or three hundred people; all of them knew why they were there. All of a sudden, I heard someone calling, "Shlomo!" I was surprised and turned around to see who had recognized me. Then the voice repeated, "Shlomo! Don't you recognize me?" After looking more closely at the man who had called me, I finally recognized my father's cousin, Leon Venezia. His voice had changed and he was nothing but skin and bone. He'd been deported in the same transport as had I, but hadn't been selected for the Sonderkommando. He told me he'd been working at building water channels. He'd banged his knee. His knee had swollen up and he'd been taken to hospital. But the hospital wasn't a place where you got cured – if you weren't better naturally after a few days, you risked being selected for the gas chamber. This, unfortunately, was what had happened to him; without any first aid, his knee had swollen up and they'd taken him during the selection. He begged me to go and talk to the SS-Unterscharführer who was standing guard, to try to convince the guard to take him into the Sonderkommando. I tried to explain to him that there was no point, since we were all in the same situation. But he insisted – and so, to calm him down, I did go to see the German. He waved me away, "*Ah! Das ist scheißegal!*" "I don't give a shit!" I went back to Leon and, to take his mind off the situation, asked whether he was hungry. I knew he certainly wouldn't have eaten anything much for a long time. He said yes, of course. I ran to fetch a hunk of bread and some canned sardines from under my bed, and I rushed back over so as not to run the risk that he'd already have been [gassed before I could get back with the food]. . . . I gave him everything. He didn't even take the time to chew it, he swallowed it all as if it were water, he was so famished. Then his turn came to enter the gas chamber. He was among the last to go in and the German started yelling. I took him by the arm as he continued asking me all those questions that I found so upsetting: "How long does it take to die? Does it really hurt?" I didn't know what to tell him, so I lied and said it didn't take long, it didn't hurt. In reality, ten to twelve minutes gasping for air is a long time, but I told him lies to set his mind at rest, to reassure him. The German started shouting again, so we gave each other a hug and he went in. He was the last to enter and the German closed the door behind him. My comrades supported me and took me away so that I wouldn't have to see the moment when they opened the door of the gas chamber. It was already hard enough to see him like that. When they brought him to the ovens, the men called my brother and me so we could recite *kaddish* before burning his body.

There's another episode I have to relate. One day, while I was presenting my testimony at a school, a young girl asked me if anyone had ever emerged from the gas chamber alive. Her schoolmates laughed at her, as if she hadn't understood a thing. How could anyone survive in those conditions, when

the deadly gas used had been carefully developed to kill everyone? It's impossible. In spite of everything, however absurd
her question may seem, it was quite relevant, since it did
indeed happen.

Few people ever saw and can relate this episode, and yet it
is true. One day when everyone had started working normally
after the arrival of a transport, one of the men involved in
removing the bodies from the gas chamber heard a strange
noise. It wasn't so unusual to hear strange noises, since sometimes the victims' bodies continued to emit gas. But this
time he claimed the noise was different. We stopped and
pricked up our ears, but nobody could hear anything. We told
ourselves that he'd surely been hearing voices. A few minutes
later, he again stopped and told us that this time he was certain he'd heard a death rattle. And when we listened closely,
we, too, could hear the same noise. It was a sort of wailing. To
begin with, the sounds were spaced out, then they came more
frequently until they became a continuous crying that we all
identified as the crying of a newborn baby. The man who had
heard it first went to see where exactly the noise was coming
from. Stepping over the bodies, he found the source of those
little wailings. It was a baby girl, barely two months old, still
clinging to her mother's breast and vainly trying to suckle. She
was crying because she could feel that the milk had stopped
flowing. He took the baby and brought it out of the gas chamber. We knew it would be impossible to keep her with us.
Impossible to hide her or get her accepted by the Germans.
And indeed, as soon as the guard saw the baby, he didn't seem
at all displeased at having a little baby to kill. He fired a shot
and that little girl who had miraculously survived the gas was
dead. Nobody could survive. Everybody had to die, including
us: it was just a matter of time.

Some years ago, I had the opportunity of asking the head
of the largest pediatric hospital in Rome how he could explain

this phenomenon. He told me it was not impossible that the child, as she suckled, was insulated by the strength with which she was sucking at her mother's breast, which would have limited the absorption of the deadly gas.

Do you remember any other people, the faces of any others whom you saw before their death?

Yes, I remember a man of about forty who arrived in a transport of deportees from Belgium. He happened to be in the autopsy room, sitting on the big slab of stone. I caught sight of him by chance, as I passed the room – its door had been left ajar. I immediately saw that one whole side of his face and his neck was wounded, torn, bloody. As soon as he saw me, he said, in French: "I want to die." "What have you done?" I asked, pointing to his face. He explained that he had attempted suicide with a razor blade, in the train. You could see his carotid, but he hadn't slit the right veins and the attempt hadn't been fatal. The Germans had put him in here until they decided what to do with him. I suppose they executed him shortly afterwards. I never saw him again.

Is it the autopsy room in Crematorium II that you mean?

No. It's true that the autopsy room was in Crematorium II. In III, which was identical, but constructed as a mirror of II, the autopsy room was actually used to melt gold. There was a table, and generally there were two Czech Jews designated specially to melt gold; they made ingots from the jewelry and gold teeth found on the victims. That was the room in which I saw the man.

I never went into the real autopsy room, in Crematorium II, because I never had any particular reason to go into that room. But once, when I happened to be in Crematorium II, the body of a Russian officer was brought in to be analyzed by Dr. Nyiszli, the Jewish Hungarian doctor, Mengele's assistant. Several SS officers were there to attend the autopsy. I suppose Mengele was one of them, but I wouldn't have been able to recognize him. When they finished, the corpse needed to be carried to the ovens. The poor man's stomach was still open, with his bowels hanging out. Nothing shocked us anymore, but seeing his intestine trailing down to the ground and dragging along for seven or eight meters is an image that stayed in my mind.

I also remember the arrival of an unusual transport of Italians. I suppose they were Italians, but I saw them only when they arrived on the ramp; they hadn't been sent to my crematorium. This was fortunate, since it would have been a horrible experience for me to see Italians or Greeks being sent to be gassed in my crematorium. I deduced that they were Italians from the fact that the transport was accompanied by soldiers wearing fezzes and pompons characteristic of the Italian military uniform and they carried rifles. When the train arrived, the Germans didn't immediately open the doors to let out the deportees. The Jews stayed in the train, while the Germans assembled the Italian soldiers, twenty or twenty-five of them, in rows, by twos. The SS took them through the *Lagerstrasse*. I don't know what exactly happened to them, but I imagine they joined the prisoners of war, unless they were executed. I never heard any more about them. It was only once the Italians had left that the Jewish deportees were disembarked from the train and sent to their deaths in one of the other crematoria.[1]

---

[1] The fact that Italian guards, set to keep watch over the transports, reached the interior, on the *Bahnrampe*, is also reported in eye-witness accounts by other Italian survivors, especially the ones set to work on the ramp.

◀ *Shlomo (age twenty) at Athens in 1944, a few weeks before his deportation. (D.R.)*

▶ *Portrait of Shlomo at Auschwitz, wearing the blue and white scarf of former deportees (March 2003). (D.R.)*

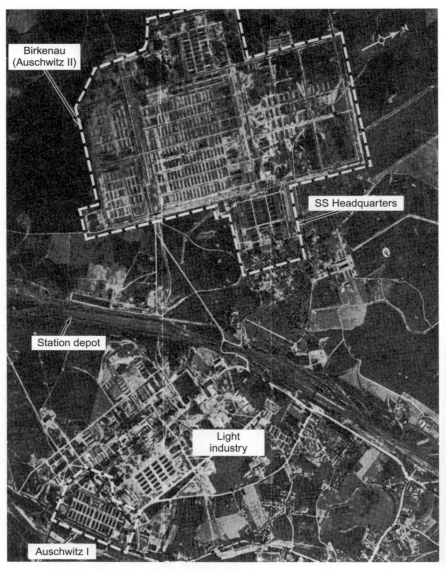

▲ *Aerial view of part of the Auschwitz complex with Auschwitz I and Auschwitz II-Birkenau. The railway situated between the two camps, the Judenrampe, was used as an arrival and selection ramp for transports of Jews until May 1944, when it was replaced by the Bahnrampe, which brought victims right into the camp, near Crematoria II and III. (Mémorial de la Shoah/CDJC.)*

▶ *Aerial photo taken by the RAF on a reconnaissance mission over Birkenau, August 23, 1944. At the top of the picture, smoke is rising from the mass graves of Crematorium V. (The Aerial Reconnaissance Archives.)*

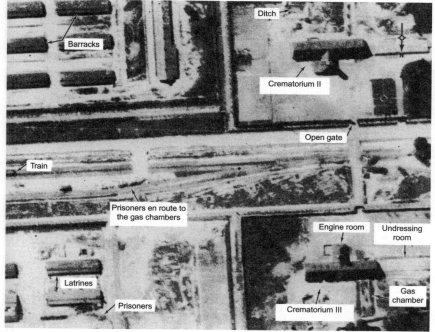

▲ *Detailed view of Crematoria II and III at Birkenau, annotated by Jean-Claude Pressac. (Mémorial de la Shoah/CDJC.)*

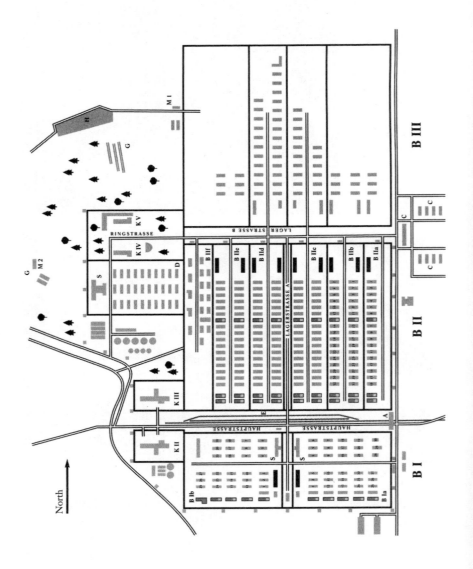

North

▲ *This snapshot is one of a series of five photographs secretly taken by someone called "Alex," an unidentified member of the resistance network at Auschwitz. Taken from inside Crematorium V in August 1944, it shows (here in detail) the naked women entering the gas chamber of Crematorium V, after undressing in the open air. (Archive of the Auschwitz-Birkenau State Museum.)*

◀ *Plan of Auschwitz-Birkenau
(Yad Vashem/Fondation pour la Mémoire de la Shoah.)*

A	*main guard service with watch tower*	*D*	*storage area for objects pillaged from*
BI	*first sector of the camp*		*murdered prisoners (Kanada)*
BII	*second sector of the camp*	*E*	*ramp where the transports were unloaded*
BIII	*third sector of the camp, under construction*		*and selection took place*
	(Mexico)	*G*	*pyres where corpses were burned*
BIa	*women's camp*	*H*	*mass graves for Soviet prisoners of war*
BIb	*initially, men's camp; from 1943, women's*	*K II*	*Crematorium II gas chamber and ovens*
	camp	*K III*	*Crematorium III gas chamber and ovens*
BIIa	*quarantine camp*	*K IV*	*Crematorium IV gas chamber and ovens*
BIIb	*family camp for the Jews from*	*K V*	*Crematorium V gas chamber and ovens*
	Theresienstadt	*M 1*	*first provisional gas chamber (white house)*
BIIc	*camp for the Jews from Hungary*	*M 2*	*second provisional gas chamber (red house)*
BIId	*men's camp*	*S*	*showers and registration (Sauna)*
BIIe	*Gypsies' camp (Zigeunerlager)*		
BIIf	*prisoners' hospital*	▮	*Latrines and washbasins*
C	*Kommandantur and barracks for the SS*		

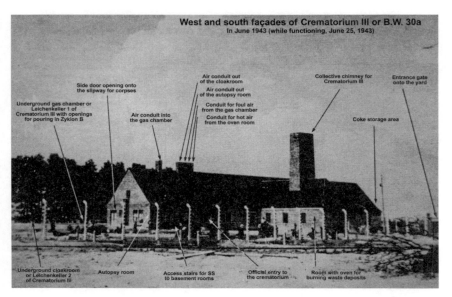

West and south façades of Crematorium III or B.W. 30a
In June 1943 (while functioning, June 25, 1943)

Side door opening onto
the slipway for corpses

Underground gas chamber or
Leichenkeller 1 of
Crematorium III with openings
for pouring in Zyklon B

Air conduit into
the gas chamber

Air conduit out
of the cloakroom

Air conduit out
of the autopsy room

Conduit for foul air
from the gas chamber

Conduit for hot air
from the oven room

Collective chimney for
Crematorium III

Entrance gate
onto the yard

Coke storage area

Underground cloakroom
or Leichenkeller 2
of Crematorium III

Autopsy room

Access stairs for SS
to basement rooms

Official entry to
the crematorium

Room with oven for
burning waste deposits

▲ *Photo of Crematorium III, annotated by Jean-Claude Pressac. (CNRS Éditions, 1993, APMO 20995/507.)*

▲ *Visualization of Crematorium II. In basement on left, the room for undressing. On the right side, also in the basement, the gas chamber. (Klarsfeld Foundation.)*

▲ *From* The Auschwitz Album, *a photo taken by an SS officer on the arrival of a transport of Jews from Hungary. Behind the people being sent to Crematorium II, the façade of the oven room of Crematorium III is perfectly visible. (Public domain/Fondation pour la Mémoire de la Shoah.)*

◄ *General view of the ovens of Crematorium II a few weeks before it started to operate. (The archival collection of the Auschwitz-Birkenau State Museum in Oświęcim.)*

◄ *Ruins of Crematorium II at the Liberation. In the foreground, tree trunks had been piled up at the end of summer 1944 to camouflage the spot. (Mémorial de la Shoah/CDJC.)*

Shlomo bearing witness in front of the ruins of Crematorium II at Birkenau. Next to him, historian Marcello Pezzetti, who specializes in Auschwitz (March 2004). (Sara Berger.)

Shlomo and Avraham Dragon (also a former member of the Sonderkommando), Israel, July 2004. (Marcello Pezzetti.)

Shlomo and Lemke (Chaim) Pliszko (member of the Sonderkommando and former kapo of Crematorium II), Israel, July 2004. (Marcello Pezzetti.)

From left to right: Avraham Dragon, his brother Shlomo Dragon, Eliezer Eisenschmidt, Yakob Gabbai, Josef Sackar (behind), and Shaul Hazan at Birkenau. (Marcello Pezzetti.)

Shlomo (right) with his brother Maurice Venezia (left) and his cousin Dario Gabbai (center). (Marcello Pezzetti.)

Did you see any Gypsies in your crematorium?

No; they weren't sent to my crematorium. I think that, when the Gypsy camp was liquidated, they were sent to Crematorium IV to be gassed.[2] It all happened at night. Although my crematorium was very close to their camp, I didn't see or hear anything when this sector was liquidated.

In any case, I never saw any non-Jews being gassed. I know the Gypsies were sent to the gas chamber, but I didn't see them. The only non-Jews I ever saw in the Crematorium were the Russians who were with us in the Sonderkommando, but they didn't even work. Once, too, I met a young non-Jewish Pole, a woman, inside the Crematorium. She was a resistance fighter who'd been arrested for blowing up a train, or trying to, I'm not sure. She was captured alive and brought to the Crematorium. The Germans left her in the chimney room while working out what to do with her. I went in by chance and saw her by the window. When she saw me, she started to yell in Polish, *"Zyd!"* terror-stricken. I soon realized she wasn't all that fond of Jews. . . . So I didn't insist, and closed the door behind me to leave her alone. I'd like to have helped her, but she didn't seem to want me to. I don't know what happened to her after that, but she probably was executed with a bullet through the back of the neck.

[2] The first Roma and Sinti (Gypsies) deported to Auschwitz-Birkenau arrived in the camp at the beginning of December 1942, even before the December 16, 1942 publication of Himmler's decree setting out the arrangements for the deportation of Gypsies to the camp there. From February 1943 onwards, they were systematically incorporated into the camp without undergoing selection, and maintained in Sector BIIe (*Zigeuner-lager*: Gypsy camp). On March 22, 1943, a first *Aktion* put to death one thousand, seven hundred Gypsies suspected of having typhus. Five hundred others were gassed in May. Between May and August 1944, several Gypsies were transferred to camps inside the Reich. Those who remained (2,897 in total) were eliminated in the gas chambers at Birkenau on the night of August 2–3, 1944, when the *Zigeunerlager* was liquidated.

What were relations like with the non-Jewish Polish prisoners?

In Birkenau, I didn't really ever meet any, apart from the terrible kapo in quarantine. But I do know that the preparations
for the Sonderkommando revolt were carried out in coordi-
nation with the Polish Resistance both inside and outside the
camp. But there was a rumor going around that the members
of the resistance on the outside were dragging things out as
long as possible and taking advantage to keep asking for more
money to buy weapons. What is certain is they were forever
delaying the outbreak of the revolt. For us, each wasted day
corresponded to hundreds of additional victims and also to the
approach of our own certain end. For them, each extra day
they got through corresponded to money to get weapons and
a greater hope of being saved by the advance of the Soviet
troops. But if we'd had to wait for the Russians, the revolt
wouldn't have happened before December: it was only then
that we began to hear the sound of approaching artillery.

5

THE REVOLT OF THE
SONDERKOMMANDO AND THE
DISMANTLING OF THE CREMATORIA

The idea of the revolt already had been around long before I entered the camp. It had managed to survive despite various selections, and thanks to certain kapos such as Lemke or Kaminski who had been there for a long time and had taken over the organization of the revolt. Kaminski was the head of the kapos in the crematoria, but he was also the main brains behind the revolt and a man whom everyone respected. He and a few others managed to establish contact with the outside and to coordinate a small group of people involved in organizing the revolt. Contacts took place, as I've said, either when it was time to get the soup, or in the women's camp, to which certain men from the Sonderkommando did, in exceptional cases, have access. Their job was to transmit money that went through several hands before it reached the resistance fighters outside the camp. One of the men who established these contacts was called Alter. He was a Polish Jew, very tall and rather pretentious – I fought him, on one occasion, over a cap that he wouldn't give back to a friend of mine. I found out only later why he went so often into the women's camp and the kitchen. He was, in fact, going to pick up the explosive powder that Jewish women prisoners working in the factory near the camp procured for him.[1]

I myself was too young and had arrived too recently to be told about these preparations. Like all the other men in the Sonderkommando, I was informed only at the last moment. I didn't suspect a thing. Everything needed to be kept secret, otherwise one of us might weaken and go tell the Germans what he knew in the hope of saving his own skin. Everything was done with the utmost discretion and the kapos trusted only experienced men. It was only two days before the outbreak of the revolt that it became obvious that something was in the offing. But nobody dared talk openly about it. It was in the air, but not confirmed.

On the day before the revolt was due to start (I think it was a Friday, but I know that others say it was a Saturday), we were individually alerted by our kapo. The main part of the revolt was to take place in Crematorium II. Every day, at around six in the evening, SS guards passed by the main entrance to Crematorium II to take up their positions in the closed watchtowers where they spent the night. They marched in a relaxed fashion, unhurriedly, with their sub-machine guns shouldered, and we sometimes heard them laughing and joking with each other. The plan was that just as they were passing, some men would open the big gate and jump out at the Germans to kill them and grab their weapons. This moment would be the signal for the revolt in all the other crematoria.

Everything had been programmed down to the last detail. In the end, it had been decided not to bother with the

---

[1] Róza Robota, Ella Gärtner, Ester Wajcblum, and Regina Safirsztain, who worked in the Kanada and the Weichsel-Union, were publicly hanged by the Nazis on January 6, 1945 for passing gunpowder to the members of the Sonderkommando.

resistance fighters outside the camp, since they refused to agree on a date. In my view, the revolt was triggered by the Sonderkommando just then because it seemed obvious that the last convoys from Hungary were arriving and very soon there would be nobody left to gas. Then it would be our turn. We had to make one last attempt. Even if the hope was in vain, we were all convinced that it would be better to act and get killed rather than die without having made any attempt.

Lemke had told us to get ready, but he didn't use the word "revolt." He merely said: "Get ready, we're going to do something to try to get out of here."

So I set aside a jacket and a pair of trousers that would be of use to me when I escaped. In general, we had to make a hole in the back and on the side of our trousers to sew in its place a piece of striped cloth with our number. But on this occasion I didn't make a hole, I merely sewed the striped cloth, so that I could tear it easily and pass unnoticed once I was outside the camp. I hid these clothes in the room that was used to store coal.

Did you hope that the plan would work?

Yes, of course, everybody thought it would. Our hope was not so much to survive as to do something, to rise up, so as not to keep on as we were. It was obvious that some of us would perish in the attempt. But whether we died or not, revolt was imperative. Nobody wondered whether it was really going to work or not; the important thing was to do something!

The revolt was to start at six in the evening. That day, at around two in the afternoon, a transport of deportees arrived on the ramp. There were quite a few of them. Normally, barely half an hour after the arrival of a transport, the train guards were replaced by SS who opened the boxcars and brought the prisoners to the *Sauna* or the crematoria. But on this occasion, there was no movement, nobody came. We couldn't understand why this transport was just left there without anyone bothering about it. Later on, we found out that, at the same moment, an SS officer and two non-commissioned officers had gone to Crematorium IV and called two hundred Sonderkommando men by their numbers, ordering them to come down. The men who were getting ready to stage the revolt thought the Germans were starting to be suspicious and wanted to eliminate them before the revolt broke out. Nobody agreed to come down.

All this we found out only later, through one of the men who was there: Isaac Venezia (another Venezia, but he wasn't a member of my family, either). He'd managed to get across to our crematorium. I myself didn't see him, but my brother personally told me what he had heard. He said that the men of Crematorium IV had set fire to the mattresses and thereby triggered the revolt before the scheduled time, convinced as they were that someone had betrayed them. It seems they'd had time to kill three Germans before reinforcements arrived. They set fire to the Crematorium and tried to escape. But almost all were killed on the spot.

From our crematorium, it was possible to see a strange cloud of smoke rising from Crematorium IV. But we were too far away and had no means of communication to understand what was happening. A German set off the alarm bell and very soon we were all shut off inside the crematorium where we worked. The situation was pretty much the same in Crematorium II, except for the fact that, from there, many men tried to escape. Unfortunately they didn't get very far.

Personally, I didn't immediately see what was happening. Lemke had told me to go down into the basement with one of the Russians and wait for the German guard. It was all as scheduled, but he hadn't told me exactly what I was supposed to do. We went down. The Russian lit up a cigarette and suddenly brought out from under his clothes a dagger and an ax and showed them to me, gesturing to me to choose between them. I immediately realized what was going to happen and seized the ax. It appeared easier to strike with an ax. I'd never done so, but I had to do it, so I reflected that an ax kept you at a greater distance from the victim than did the dagger. Clutching this ax and trembling with fear, I had to wait until the German came down. The guard, that day, was the man who so enjoyed killing people. Our kapo was to tell him that a water pipe in the basement had gotten clogged and that he needed to come down and take a look. But he never did come down, since he must have been warned of what was happening in Crematorium IV and must have suspected that we were laying a trap for him.

So we waited there for over two hours, weapons in hand. Finally, one of our friends came down, whistling. This was the agreed signal so that we wouldn't think he was the guard. He informed us that the plan had failed and told us to go back up to where the others were. Everything was abuzz: the Germans had already occupied the yard.

What did you know about what was happening at the same time in Crematorium IV?

Nothing; we found out only the next day what had happened, since the SS had encircled our crematorium and were preventing anyone from leaving. They were wearing combat uniforms and carrying heavy machine guns like the ones they carried for warfare. Lemke saved our lives by telling us not to move. In Crematorium II, all of those who tried to escape were killed. If he hadn't been so firm, some men probably would have tried to force the gates open in turn. But we stayed put.

The SS man who was on duty in our crematorium, and had soon fled when he realized he risked being killed, came back with reinforcements. He summoned the Russian who generally looked after the maintenance of his bicycle. With the revolt in mind, the Russian had punctured the bicycle wheels to slow the German should he try to inform the *Kommandantur*. When he realized this, the German went wild and beat the Russian to death in front of us. I felt relieved about at least one thing: I'd had time, on coming back up from the basement, to go around the Crematorium and pick up the clothes I'd hidden in the coal store. I immediately tore off the number I'd sewn on, since if they'd discovered it without a hole and with my number on it, they'd have realized that I'd been intending to escape.

We passed the whole night without moving. They didn't come in.

The next day, the Germans demanded that thirty men come out to finish the work that hadn't been completed in Crematorium II. I decided to join this group of thirty men, since I'd lost all hope of surviving otherwise. The soldiers still had the Crematorium surrounded, and it was merely a question of time before they attacked if we didn't come out of our own free will. Contrary to what I'd been expecting, they didn't kill us on the spot. We were sent to Crematorium II. There, two or three prisoners who hadn't tried to escape were still alive and told us what had happened. At that time, we still didn't know that all of the others, those who'd tried to escape, already had been recaptured and killed. These prisoners told us what they'd done with that man Karol, the German kapo who was a common law criminal and had, it appears, denounced and revealed the projected revolt. The prisoners beat him and threw him into the oven fully clothed, just as he was.

We set back to work to burn the bodies that had been left in the gas chamber. That evening, our relief should have arrived to take over from us. But we worked a thirty-six-hour shift without anybody bothering to come. Finally, they allowed us to go up and get some rest. It was just then that the bodies of the escaped prisoners were laid out in the yard of the Crematorium before being carried to the ovens to be burned. But it was other prisoners who did so. They didn't want it to be men from the Sonderkommando who burned the bodies of their own comrades, in case this might inspire a second revolt. Subsequently, the last men who had refused to leave Crematorium III at the same time as we had stayed put finally were transferred to Crematorium II, where they came to join us.

Crematorium III was no longer used after that, and the Germans started to dismantle it shortly after the revolt. Crematorium IV was already out of action, since the Sonderkommando men had managed to blow it up during the revolt. It was the beginning of October 1944, and only Crematorium II was still operating. But not as quickly as before; the transports no longer arrived so regularly.

So you weren't subjected to any real reprisals?

We were convinced that we would be, that the Germans were using us because they still needed us, but that it wouldn't be long. I don't know how many men still were alive in Crematoria IV and V, but there can't have been many of them. We were practically the only ones still left alive.

The Germans drew up a list of the living and the dead, and concluded that two people were missing. They brought over Kaminski, the *Oberkapo* of the crematoria, to find out who and where the missing persons were. One was Ivan, a Russian, and the other was Karol, the German. Kaminski had to explain what had happened with Karol and say that he had been burned. The Germans couldn't believe it. Then, to prove that it was true, it was necessary to sort through the ashes, rummage around among them until the searchers found the metal buttons that Karol always wore on his jacket. Later, we discovered that the Germans had come for Kaminski around four in the morning. They took him away, and we never saw him again.

Ivan was still missing, and so long as he wasn't found, the alarm bell continued to ring for a long time without stopping. Ivan was eventually found in a small village, two weeks later. He was brought back alive and killed in the Crematorium. All the other Russians were transferred elsewhere. We were alone in the Crematorium and the Germans started to keep us under strict surveillance. We lost any bit of freedom we once had inside the Crematorium. They even brought in reinforcements of German soldiers to keep guard over us. This was the first time these soldiers had entered the Crematorium yard. Among them, I noticed an SS man who seemed curious to see what was inside. He hesitated, as he probably had no authorization. All the same, he went down there, and then came straight back up. I suppose he didn't go any farther than the undressing room. He didn't see any corpses. He wanted to know, but he didn't see anything.

Apart from keeping you under closer surveillance, they didn't impose any other punishment on you?

A few days later, an officer and two soldiers came into our crematorium. They sounded the assembly bell and made us go into the room with the ovens in groups of five. As we stood waiting at the door, all of us were convinced that they were going to kill us. We couldn't hear what was going on inside and we couldn't see anybody coming out. I went and stood among the last in the queue. As I always did, in fact, since in those cases I prefer to have time to understand what's happening so that I can prepare myself as much as possible. I smoked the last cigarettes I had, out of anxiety and despair. We'd arranged with the ones going in first that if they saw they were going to be killed, they'd start to shout to warn us. We would have done something, out of despair, without the slightest chance of escaping, but just so we wouldn't be led like sheep to the slaughter.

When it was our turn to go in, they ordered us to form four groups of five prisoners and to stand in front of the ovens. Each of the two SS men stood at one of the two corners of the room that were facing us. The officer was in the middle, giving orders. He ordered us to get undressed. I told myself: "This is it. It's all over!" Then he ordered us to place our things in a bundle a couple of yards in front of us. So we stood there, motionless, naked, sweating, waiting to see what he was going to do. Two Germans came into the room and searched all the clothes. Then, when they realized that we had no knives, revolvers, or anything of the kind, they ordered us to get dressed again. And we had to get on with our work.

You said that the transports had practically stopped arriving. What were you doing at that time?

Towards the end of October, the order came to start dismantling the crematoria. We continued to work occasionally in Crematorium II, when a transport did arrive in spite of everything. It was this crematorium that stayed active the longest, burning the last corpses. But we worked mainly at dismantling the other crematoria. This took a considerable time, since the Germans ordered us to take everything apart bit by bit. The structures were very solid and had been built to last a long time. They could have used dynamite just as well, but they wanted to disassemble the whole inside of the structures methodically: the ovens, the doors of the gas chamber, and all the rest. And this needed to be done by men from the

Sonderkommando, since we were the only ones allowed to see the inside of the gas chambers. On the other hand, when the outer structure was dismantled, other prisoners, including women from Birkenau and prisoners from Auschwitz I, were set to work at this task.

From time to time I managed to slip into the group of those who were working outside, dismantling the exterior structure. This enabled me to get a bit of fresh air and to try to get some news of people I knew. One day, as I was outside with a group dismantling a guard turret, I drove a rusty nail into my hand. At the beginning, the pain was tolerable. But the wound rapidly got infected. The pain ran all the way up my arm, right to my armpit, where the glands swelled up and hurt dreadfully. I was running a fever, but men from the Sonderkommando couldn't go to the hospital like the others. A Jewish doctor in the Sonderkommando team told me he'd have to open the wound to evacuate the pus.

So he took a scalpel and sat me down on a chair. Three or four men took firm hold of me, for there was, of course, no anesthetic. Just as the doctor was about to operate, we heard the sounds of shooting coming from the Crematorium yard. Those who could went over to the window and saw a van transporting six or seven Russians who had been brought from Auschwitz I to our crematorium. Thinking they were going to be killed, the Russians flung themselves at the soldiers as they left the wagon. Faced with the Germans, there weren't enough of them, and they were cut down like dogs. I remember thinking: "I'm ill, but I'm going to be cured, while those men are in good health and are being cut down like animals."

The doctor carried on; he opened my arm and I saw stars! A great deal of pus came out. There wasn't any bandage to dress the wound, but they'd found some toilet paper among the different things that came in with the victims. This served as a bandage, with a bit of eau de Cologne as alcohol to disinfect the wound. I recovered in a few days, as I was still quite strong. Obviously, it really wasn't possible for me to say that I was ill. Luckily, the work just then wasn't as back-breaking, and so I was able to avoid using my hand and thereby showing that I had a problem.

Did you have any news about people you knew?

Yes, among the prisoners who came to dismantle the crematoria, I came across my brother-in-law, who had been escorting a group of prisoners from Auschwitz I. He was a good woodworker and, as he had been in the camp for a long time, he'd managed to get himself a position that provided him with several advantages. He could have stayed away from this work, but he, too, wanted to understand what was happening in these structures and to try to get some news of us. He'd already managed to find my sister and even to get her a safe place in a kommando of seamstresses. When I saw him, I asked him to give to my sister a small bag that I'd found: it contained several gold teeth. . . .

I'd found them when I was rummaging round in the Crematorium yard. It was well known that men from the Sonderkommando were in the habit of burying various valuable objects for safekeeping. We on our side didn't have much left, since the convoys had stopped arriving and we couldn't put aside enough food. So I came to an agreement with another Greek from Salonika, Shaul Hazan; he was to be my *Shutaf*, in other words my "partner" in our searches. Everything we found, we automatically divided between the two of us. While the one searched, the other kept a lookout. In this way, by digging around in the ground, he found a bag filled with gold teeth. We immediately hid it in another place. From time to time we'd go and fetch one of the teeth, which we then exchanged for a hunk of bread.

My searches were rewarded too. I remembered that the German guard of Crematorium II still had a dog. One day, the dog went too close to the electrified barbed-wire fence, and was killed. For the German, the death of this dog was a real tragedy – the life of a dog was worth more in his eyes than the lives of a thousand Jews. That day he took it out on us – he didn't give us a moment's respite. He finally ordered the Russians to stuff the dog. The dog's flesh didn't all end up in the garbage; I know that several prisoners ate it. Even my brother took a taste.

The German had had a very fine kennel built for his dog in the yard of Crematorium II. It looked like a little brick house, with a small carpet at the entrance. This kennel had to go too, since the whole crematorium was being dismantled. I took considerable satisfaction in destroying that kennel. I waded in with a pickax. I wanted to kill everybody, smash everything; anything I could destroy in that place made me happy, I wanted to be done with that place. Destroy as much as possible. . . . We didn't know what they could still do to us, so the more we destroyed, the better we felt. That dog had had the right to more respect and comfort than we had. I was happy to smash up its kennel. The ground inside the kennel was covered with bricks. I smashed them one by one, and then I suddenly noticed something hidden underneath, gleaming. When I pulled the bricks away, I discovered a magnificent gold cigarette case. On the one side, a mechanism transformed the cigarette case into a lighter. I opened it; inside, I found a thousand-dollar bill folded up. I'd never seen such a thing! I immediately went to show my discovery to my *Shutaf* and we hid it somewhere else in the yard.

On the day I saw my brother-in-law, I decided to give him my part of the booty to help my sister. I went to tell Shaul as much. He tried to dissuade me. He was worried that somebody might see us and find the place we'd hidden it. I insisted and he eventually had to give in. Unfortunately, he was right, as someone had indeed seen us and when, later, he went back to get his own portion of the spoils, there was nothing left.

I gave my portion of the gold teeth to my sister. I really wanted to help her so she'd have enough to eat and hence enough strength not to get sick. I'd already exchanged the cigarette case for two bread rolls, a piece of sausage, and – that was all. That tells you how expensive a bit of food was in the camp. . . . At least that enabled us to survive for a few days longer.

At that time the remaining men of the Sonderkommando had to come back to sleep in the men's camp as soon as the dismantling had reached the roof of the Crematorium. So we went back to the isolated barrack in the men's camp, where we had spent our first nights as members of the Sonderkommando. There were hardly seventy of us in the barrack, so we didn't lack space to keep our things. It still was strictly forbidden for us to make any contact with the other prisoners. In general, the SS brought us back to the entrance to the men's camp sector and gave one of us the task of ensuring that nobody left the barrack. If, in spite of everything, anyone did leave, the man charged with standing guard was severely punished also.

Quite unusually, on the evening of January 17, the SS guard accompanied us to the barrack and told us that we were strictly forbidden to leave. He even added, as if we didn't know this already, "Really bad things will happen to anyone who even tries!" The fact that he felt it necessary to add something that was so obvious to all of us struck us as suspect – especially since on that day, as we came back to the barrack, we crossed the path of several lines of prisoners leaving the camp as if they were going off to work, even though night was falling (it must have been around six in the evening). On the road, I managed to ask someone, discreetly, "*Was ist?*" "What's happening?" He whispered back to me, "*Evakuieren!*" It wasn't hard for me to realize that, if everyone other than the Sonderkommando was being evacuated, and we were being strictly ordered not to move, they must be intending to trap us like mice and kill us. We went into the barrack, but no sooner had the German gone away than we came out again and mingled discreetly with the groups leaving the camp. . . .

Several groups, each one of several thousand prisoners, had been formed, since it was impossible to send everyone to the same place. To begin with, we were sent to Auschwitz I, where we joined other prisoners who were also ready to be evacuated. Night was already far gone. I found my brother-in-law in Auschwitz I, as well as other prisoners I knew, such as my brother-in-law's cousin, Joseph Mano, and others too. Everyone was given three portions of bread with a little bit of margarine for the road. To preclude anyone stealing mine, I elected to swallow the whole ration immediately and ensure that I'd have at least that in my belly.

It was midwinter; outside, everything was frozen or covered in snow. It was beastly cold. But I was happy knowing that I was going to leave that place behind, and especially that I'd managed to escape the liquidation planned for the Sonderkommando. From time to time, during the night, a German passed among the prisoners and yelled, "*Wer hat im Sonderkommando gearbeitet?*" "Who worked in the Sonderkommando?" Of course, nobody replied. Later on, they continued to ask the question regularly, all along the road, since they had no other means of identifying us. That night, the one preceding what was called "the death march," I didn't sleep at all. There wasn't enough room for everybody and I spent the night huddled against the others, standing up. Even so, I was lucky enough to manage to get inside a building, since some people spent the night outside.

The next morning, we left Auschwitz. In my column, there must have been five or six thousand of us. We marched for

days on end, always five by five, through that icy cold. At
night, we arrived in a village or a cowshed, and we had to do
what little we could to find a decent place to rest for a while.
The ones with the most practical sense managed to find a
place indoors; the others had to stay outside. Many died of
cold during the night, or their feet got frozen. If they could no
longer walk, they were killed on the spot. We were dragging
our feet, we were thirsty, cold, hungry . . . but we had to
march, march, and keep on marching. Those who dropped
from exhaustion were left behind and were executed by the SS
who brought up the rear. Other prisoners had to throw their
bodies into the ditches.

This lasted some ten or twelve days.

Did you encounter any civilians on the road?

Yes, frequently, even though the Germans avoided taking us
through towns and preferred back roads on which we only
ever saw isolated farms. The inhabitants watched us pass; they,
too, were certainly terrified. I would like to have paid better
thanks to an old Polish woman we met on the second day. She
threw three or four big loaves of bread to us. I was one of the
lucky ones who managed to grab one. It was strictly forbidden
by the Germans, but for as long as she could do so, she continued throwing them, then she walked away.

On several occasions, I managed to pick up things on the
road; otherwise I wouldn't have been able to survive. One
evening, for example, we stopped in a barn. When I went in,
I saw a little trapdoor on the ground. I smashed it open so I
could climb down into the hole. I had to clamber down but
I couldn't make out a thing. I told my brother and [my
cousin] Yakob to hold me by my hands and to let me slip
down gently. It wasn't all that deep, and the others came
down and joined me. The peasant had rigged out a little

cellar just under the ground to store his potatoes under some sand. As soon as we saw the potatoes, we pounced on them and ate them up.

On another occasion, I slept in a cowshed, on some straw. The place was quite big and the straw kept us a bit warmer. We were absolutely dead-tired and without strength, but the Germans let us sleep for only a few hours, before making us set off again at dawn. This time, a few of us had decided to stay hidden in the straw. But the Germans yelled out to warn everyone that they were going to set the cowshed on fire when they left. We ran to join the others and slipped into our places in the line.

After three or four days we reached a small country station, where open trains, like those used to transport coal, were waiting for us. In the train, we were packed in so tightly that nobody could move. It was impossible to sit down. The snow whipped into our faces as the train moved along. This lasted for two days, without a break, and nothing to eat.

It seemed obvious to everybody that the Germans would eventually just abandon us somewhere so as not to slow down their own escape. I think that's why relatively few people around us tried to escape from the Germans. Actually, some did try to escape when an opportunity presented itself. When the train stopped, a German gave permission to a few prisoners to get out of the train and relieve themselves. Several took advantage of this chance to escape, but I don't know how far they may have gotten. I didn't try anything myself, since I was sincerely convinced that they'd leave us out in the open countryside so they could get away more quickly from the advancing Soviet troops. And I was sure there wouldn't be anywhere for them to take us. I didn't want to risk being shot at by attempting to escape, and dying before the Germans left us, free. But that time never came and I spent another four months in the camps.

Did many people die on the evacuation "march"?

Yes, a huge number of people died. But I didn't necessarily see them, since people were dropping with fatigue and lying there until they were executed by the last SS in the column. There were some whom we tried to help when they were at the end of their strength. Such as the boy whose first name I've forgotten. His brother, Jacquot Maestro, was a lively, cunning youngster who'd often transmitted information to us in the camp. The boy started to vomit blood during the march. So as not to abandon him, I and another man carried him while he recovered. Those of us who came from the Sonderkommando had a bit more strength than the others, and, as much as we could, we tried to help our friends.

On the other hand, in my railcar, a man I didn't know died next to me. He was a Yugoslav; the poor man already practically looked like a skeleton. He died, but we were so crammed in together that the corpse remained standing, propped up between my brother and myself without anyone realizing. The man had died, but each of us had nearly turned into animals. My first reflex was to rummage round in his pockets, with the absurd idea in mind that he might have kept something edible in there. All I found was a wooden crucifix – I kept it, telling myself that if, by some miracle, I managed to free myself, I would be given a better reception by peasants if they didn't think I was Jewish. Then we managed to make some room to lay the corpse down on the floor so we could sit on it. The next day, when the train stopped to take on coal for the locomotive, I told the German there was a dead man in our railcar. I understood that he was telling me to chuck him off. But when we lifted the body, he told us: *"Nein! Nicht hier. Später!"* "No, not here, later!" After the train set off again, we had to throw the corpse out, since it was starting to smell bad.

The train stopped at a place where the tracks had been bombed and we continued on foot for another day. Then we embarked on freight barges on the Danube. The cold was still unbearable, but at least we had a roof over our heads. For the first time in a very long while, they handed out soup to us and we spent the night on the barge. The next morning, at around five, they made us get out and cross a bridge on which a sign said "Linz." That's how I knew we were in Austria. As we went through the town, I saw a woman taking out the rubbish bin. When I came close, I sidestepped onto the pavement and dipped my hand into the bin. I snatched out a handful of potato peelings and slipped them under my shirt. Others wanted to do the same, but a guard saw them and started beating them with the butt of his rifle. I was able to keep my peelings and eat them: they smelled awful but . . . it was still food! A little farther on, we crossed a cultivated field. With our feet, we tried to dig a bit into the soil, in the hope of finding traces of the harvest. There was a moment when I thought I'd found a whole potato: I discreetly picked it up and put it into my pocket, but it was just a stone. In the evening, we slept near a henhouse. Several of us got together to try to catch a hen, but without success. I'd have been capable of eating a hen raw if I'd been able to catch one! All the same, we did find some eggs, which we swallowed there and then. The next day, we finally reached Mauthausen.

6

MAUTHAUSEN, MELK, AND EBENSEE

I don't know exactly what day we reached Mauthausen, but I think it was the end of January. Our column of prisoners entered the camp under the enormous main gate. On the right of the door was a big building that we had to go around to reach the *Sauna*. There were still quite a few of us, in spite of the victims who had died en route: it took two days to get everyone through the Sauna. But before we went in, nobody knew what there was in the building. The prisoners had to go in in groups of five, but we didn't see them coming out again.

I slept outside for two nights so as to be among the last to go into the Sauna. I was with my brother, my cousins, and other friends from Auschwitz. Soldiers kept passing by regularly, asking *"Wer hat im Sonderkommando gearbeitet?"* To prevent them finding us, I suggested to my brother that we change our name. Instead of "Venezia," I'd say, if they asked me, that my name was "Benezia." My brother didn't want to change his name and told me it might be better if we were to separate, so that there'd be a better chance of at least one of us surviving.

Finally we went in, reassured to see that it was indeed just a Sauna for disinfection. It was on the small side. And, just as on the first day in Birkenau, we had to get completely undressed, and prisoners shaved our heads and our whole bodies. Then they gave each of us a number. But, unlike in Auschwitz, the number wasn't tattooed: Auschwitz was the only place where the prisoners were tattooed. They gave us a sort of iron bracelet with a plaque; on mine was written the number 118554. This was my identity number in Mauthausen. When they asked me my name, I said "Benezia," but they misunderstood and wrote "Benetti."

When we came out of the shower, we had to get into rows of five, naked and soaked as we were, in the snow and the cold. We had to wait until there were fifty of us in line before we could go to the barrack that was at the far end, on the left. Even if we'd been in our clothes, the cold would have been absolutely unbearable. So you can't imagine the pain of being naked, after coming out of the shower. But the man accompanying us remained impassive; he waited and forced us not to walk to the barrack too quickly. From the outside, it was similar to the ones at Birkenau, except that I seem to remember you had to go up two steps to enter. Inside there was nothing, no beds. The only positive points were the linoleum on the floor and the windows that were not broken and protected us a little from the cold.

You stayed naked, even when you slept?

Absolutely: naked and packed together like sardines, since there wasn't room for everybody. The following morning, at around ten or eleven o'clock, SS officers came looking for about three hundred people. They called us out in alphabetical order. I found myself in a group with the two Gabbai cousins, but not with my brother. They eventually sent us to another barrack to give us some clothes. We were also given some soup and then loaded onto some more railcars to be transferred to a new camp: Melk.

The journey lasted six or seven hours, no longer. The barracks were different from the ones I knew, and longer. You had to go up a few steps to get into them. There were bunk beds arranged in rows, but there weren't enough for everyone. Those who couldn't find an empty bed had problems, since no one would agree to share his place. You had to find a place somewhere in the system, even if this meant elbowing your way in. I didn't manage to get a place every day, but in general I got by reasonably well.

Work was organized in three shifts of eight hours (to which needed to be added two hours getting to the place of work and two hours getting back to the camp). When we got back, there were just as many people asleep and we had to find room somehow. You had to be strong to push others out of the way and take their place. That's why I say that solidarity did not exist. We slept on a sort of straw mattress, without undressing. If we'd taken off any item of clothing whatsoever, even our shoes, they'd have been stolen. And in order to get them back, we'd have had to pay a ration of bread.

What, exactly, was the work you did?

I worked in the kommando of masons, on a worksite belonging to some Austrian civilians. In this camp, the work consisted of building galleries into the mountain. When we arrived at the big square on the worksite, the foremen called out so many people for such-and-such a type of work. With my brother-in-law, my cousins, and friends, we managed to form a small group of fifty or so people all of whom knew each other. We contrived to stay together and always do the same work each time. The foremen and other supervisors were Austrians, but there were also SS guards and kapos. My group had to dig galleries, which had the advantage of keeping us warm and away from the German guards, who stayed outside. Austrian civilians came in from time to time to check. But in general they didn't need to come in to know whether we were working fast enough. They just needed to see the rhythm at which the conveyor belt filled with earth came out of the gallery. It was forced labor and we didn't have enough to eat or enough rest, but in other ways it wasn't too exhausting.

And the Austrian civilians – how did they treat you, in general?

They didn't give us orders, just instructions about what needed to be done. They needed a labor force, but whether we worked harder or less hard wasn't their problem. They certainly realized that some of the prisoners were so weak that they could hardly lift their arms. Sometimes they raised their voices, but they didn't use violence. Not those whom I saw, in any case. As for the others, I don't know.

But one day I was unlucky. I didn't manage to join my usual group. Someone must have slipped into the group to avoid more demanding work. So he took my place and I was forced to go and work in another kommando. I found myself in a group who worked outside, away from the gallery. We had to pull little trucks loaded with cement. When we reached the gallery, we had to push the little wagon onto a goods lift or service elevator and again push them along the tracks to the place where the prisoners needed them. This was extremely hard work.

I found myself pulling the little wagon with a non-Jewish Italian. I didn't even ask him his name; the only thing I remember is that he told me he was Sicilian. We didn't even think of talking to each other. Why waste our strength? At a certain point, I became aware that the wagon was weighing more and more heavily on my back. I stopped pulling and, as I was no longer pulling, the wagon stopped too. He was pretending to pull, but in reality he was letting me carry the whole weight of the load practically by myself. I lost my temper, as it was out of the question for me to do all the work by myself. If the chain was slowed down because of us, the German or a kapo would have come to beat us. We set off again. For the first few yards, the weight was again evenly balanced. But after a while I felt the weight growing heavier on my shoulders, and indeed, when I stopped, the wagon stopped too. Then I really did get angry and I threatened to give him a real thrashing if he let me carry the whole weight by myself again. I so longed for this day to be over and I didn't want to risk being beaten because of him! The very next day, luckily, I managed to join my usual group.

It was particularly cold during this period. The kapo in our barrack wanted us to bring back things he could burn to keep himself warm in his room. In exchange for that he would give us a little more soup. Sometimes we used the thick fabric in which the cement was transported, or else we took pieces of wood. As it was forbidden to bring anything at all into the camp, we managed to make little sections and roll them round our torsos, under our shirts. This meant we were a little less cold on the road, since the wind and the cold filtered through less easily with this bit of protection under our clothes. But one day, when we entered the camp, our group was checked over by the guards at the entrance. Everyone opened his shirt to get rid of those pieces of wood before the Germans could find them on us. If we were caught with them, we could be given a severe beating, as much as a punishment as to serve as an example to others. They'd done this so they could pick up the wood and use it for their own needs.

What did you eat?

When we set out from the camp, we were given a sort of tea, without sugar of course: the only good thing about it was that it was hot. At around eleven thirty, a kapo rang the bell for soup: a cabbage soup with potato peelings. The man serving the soup never stirred it, so the first in the queue got only water. Nobody wanted to go first. But we didn't always have any choice.

I once happened to be among the first in the soup queue. This is a very unpleasant memory. However strong and cunning I was, I fell for it. The kapo serving the soup was Hungarian and I knew he doled out much more soup to his compatriots, so I pretended I was Hungarian too. As I came up, I said to him *"Magyar!"* "Hungarian." But he easily recognized from my accent that I was lying. Instead of giving me more, he served me only water. As I stared into my tin bowl, which contained nothing substantial, I felt a great anger rising inside myself. "How could I have managed to fall so low?" The idea of having to wait another twenty-four hours before eating drove me mad. I looked to the left and the right and I discreetly tried to slip back into the queue to get another portion. But as I was trying to slip in, the prisoners who had seen me started to wave their arms and shout, "Hey! Hey there!" A kapo saw what was happening and came running towards me. As fast as I could, I tried to join the group of prisoners who had eaten already, but he didn't lose sight of me. He intended to beat me, and he rushed up, threateningly. On his way, he noticed a spade, picked it up, and gave me a great thwack on the shoulders with it. I tried to protect my head with my hands. He gave me another great thwack. If he'd stuck to the side, he'd have smashed my skull. I was left gasping for breath, filled with both pain and rage. I knew this kapo; he enjoyed killing prisoners. Often, at the entrance to the camp, he would announce proudly to the SS who were keeping an account of

those going out and coming in, "98 + 2," to show that two had
died at work, since he himself had killed those poor fellows
who were at the end of their tether. He was an Aryan Pole;
everyone was afraid of him. When he lifted the spade to hit
me a third time, I just managed to dodge the blow and I ran
away from him as fast as I could. If I'd fallen where I was, he'd
certainly have finished me off.

That day, I wept. I'd never wept in the Sonderkommando,
but all my rage welled up at just this moment. I wasn't weeping from pain or sadness (as I did after the war, when I saw
my sister again for the first time), but from anger, bitterness,
frustration . . .

How long did you stay working at Melk?

I don't know exactly, but one day they transferred us to
another sub-camp of Mauthausen: Ebensee. They chose a
group of two hundred or three hundred people. Luckily, the
little group that we had formed stayed together.

The train left us at the foot of a hill. The camp was at the
top. The barracks resembled those in Birkenau, with "bunk"
beds. There were so many of us that we had to sleep in twos.
We could hardly move, the bed was so narrow. Most of the
time, we didn't even know whom we were lying next to. There
were already a great many Frenchmen in the barrack, generally non-Jewish, as well as Russians. I found myself sharing a
bed with a sick Russian who was coughing all night long. It
was certainly because of him that I myself fell seriously ill at
the Liberation.

Did you talk to each other?

We did, but we kept conversation to a minimum. Nobody felt
much like talking. We'd come back to the barrack after a day's

exhausting work, our brains were empty, and we had nothing
to say to each other. There were a few intellectuals among us.
But we were the labor force and we'd long since lost our
dignity.

As at Melk, the work consisted in digging galleries into the
mountain. Except that we weren't digging into earth but into
stone, and the galleries were much damper than at Melk. We
were immediately soaked, whatever we did. There was no
means of getting dry. We came back to the camp and we had
to go to bed with our clothes still wet – and we couldn't take
them off. Luckily, I worked for just ten days or so in those
quarries. Subsequently, the Americans bombed the railway
station at Ebensee and then the priority was getting the prisoners to rebuild the railway line.

Every day, we had to walk to the train-stop near the camp,
then take a little train to reach the place where the tracks had
been bombed, and from there continue for another half mile
or so until we reached the bombed station at Ebensee. On the
road, we passed near a field of rapeseed plants. All the prisoners tried to pick up as much of the edible material as they possibly could. We'd have eaten grass if we'd been able to find
any. . . . But the guards soon moved in and forbade us to
approach the field. One day, we came across an old Austrian
peasant woman washing clothes in the animal trough. All the
prisoners asked her for water as they passed. She got a bucket
of water ready and placed it at the side of the road so we could
drink from it as we came by. But the Germans forbade it. With
their rifle butts they beat the old woman who had wanted to
help us.

When we reached the bombed site, we had to clear the
ground. If we were lucky, we found a cigarette butt among the
wreckage, or we found some other object that we did our best
to take back with us into the camp. Here, one of the barracks
near the latrines had become the place where we exchanged

things – did our "trading." Those who didn't work found it
easy to get there. As for us, we could go in the evenings, before
the curfew. When I could, I tried to obtain an extra hunk of
bread in exchange for a ragged cigarette butt. The Russians
were always after anything they could smoke. Once, a Russian
came to see me, and offered "*Olej!*" oil, in exchange for my
cigarettes. I knew the Russians would give anything in
exchange for something to smoke, but I wondered what on
earth it could be, since it was unthinkable that anyone might
have oil in the camp. He motioned me to wait. I was curious
to see in what sort of a container he was going to bring the oil
to me, since we never could find bottles or even bags. Finally,
he brought it to me in an oil lamp, of the kind used to light the
galleries. The oil he showed me was black, disgusting. He
tried to sell it to me by passing it off as olive oil, full of vita-
mins, while it was quite obviously motor oil. "Drink it yourself!" I replied. It may well be that some people did drink this
oil, just as some people occasionally ate the kind of whitish
cream that was found in pieces of Cardiff coal. They must
have ruined their stomachs that way.

Our kapo was a German, a small and particularly cruel man.
One day, when it was time to hand out the soup, he started to
lash out at everybody, without distinction and without reason.
One of my friends, Joseph Mano (my brother-in-law's cousin),
was hit very hard, especially on his skull. His skull was almost
smashed and nobody would have imagined that he could survive such a wound. But survive he did.

We tended to stay in a group with our own people as often
as we could, since this made us a bit stronger. If you were
alone, you were more easily someone's victim. This is what
almost happened to me, one day. It was shortly before the
Liberation. The kapos were handing out more bread. We
had to form groups of six and each group was given a big
brick-shaped hunk of bread. When I was with my brother or

other people I knew well, this was no problem: we shared the
bread very fairly. But on one occasion, I found myself,
unwillingly, in a group with five Russians, including the sick
man who shared my bunk. I very soon realized that all of
them had gotten together and were planning to cheat me.
Usually, everyone was given a number. One of the men, with
his eyes averted, designated the portion that would go to
each number. This system was fairer and prevented people
grabbing for each hunk of bread. But this time, the Russians
demanded that I be the one to turn around. When there were
only two pieces left, one for me and one for the man who
shared my bunk, I refused to turn around and told him to
choose the piece he preferred. They still insisted I turn
around. I refused, and offered him the piece that seemed the
bigger. I'd realized that, no sooner had I turned around,
they'd have taken the two pieces of bread. Things were looking ugly for me, since it was five against one. They had surely
decided to divide up my piece. And indeed, they did take
advantage of a brief lapse in attention on my part to take the
two pieces. It all happened very quickly. I saw that the
Russian who shared my bunk was still holding his bit of
bread. What could I do? Not eating was unbearable. So,
quick as a flash, I took his piece and swallowed it in a mouthful. Normally, we would try to eat in tiny little nibbles, to
give ourselves the illusion we were eating more. But now
things were really taking a turn for the worse. The Russian
who'd been left without bread started to lose his temper and
shout at me. The kapo came over and asked what was happening. The other sniveled that I'd swiped his bit of bread.
The kapo didn't ask any more questions, but started to hit me
hard. I tried to protect my face, but he hit me all over. In spite
of the force of his blows, I didn't feel any pain. My sole
thought was for the bit of bread that I'd managed to get into
my belly and that nobody would ever manage to deprive me

of! This idea was enough to lessen the pain of the blows. Eventually he got tired of hitting me and moved on to something else.

The Russian who had not had any bread went to get some from his friends. But, of course, they didn't give him any. We both continued to sleep on the same bunk, since we didn't have any choice. He couldn't do anything to get his own back: I was much stronger than he was. Anyway, he had only himself to blame.

You said you were given more bread shortly before the Liberation. Did anything else in people's attitudes or the general atmosphere change?

The kapos suddenly became less violent. The kapo in my barrack, the small, vicious German who often hit people for pleasure and without any reason, made sure he didn't get on the wrong side of the French and the Russians. He could sense that the end was near and he was afraid that we might want to take revenge as soon as we were free. All of a sudden, he became calmer and more approachable. He also tried to give more soup to the Russians and the French.

One morning, instead of us going off to work, the Ebensee commandant ordered us to assemble on the camp's central square. There must have been five or six thousand of us, from some twenty or so different camps. He got up on a podium. At his sides, interpreters translated into every language. He told us something like: "The Russians and the Americans are approaching. But we won't leave this place without putting up a fight. Your lives will be in danger in the middle of the fighting. So I recommend that you take shelter in the galleries so you won't die in the bombardments." In all languages, the prisoners shouted that they refused to do so.

Did he give you the choice?

Yes, it's strange to reflect that he did ask us the question. He could just as well have forced us to enter the galleries and killed us by blowing them up. But we'd have rebelled and that would have meant a real bloodbath. When they came in, the American troops would have found the traces of that appalling massacre. And then, the Germans didn't have time to force us. When the commandant realized that we were refusing, he gathered together his officers and they abandoned the camp. That didn't mean that we were free, since in their place there arrived men from the Wehrmacht, almost all of them rather middle-aged reservist soldiers. They were there to keep guard over us and stop us from going to plunder the village and perhaps try to take our revenge. I think we could have carried out a massacre.

Do you really think so?

Yes, we were so famished! I sincerely think we were capable of the worst just then. I'm telling you everything, and I don't want to conceal anything or tell any lies.

The guards took up their positions as they waited for the Americans. We could hear the noise of fighting in the distance. We waited like this for a day: nothing. Second day: still nothing. We didn't have anything left to eat. But not many men tried to escape, since it was just a matter of hours and it would have been idiotic to risk our lives when we were so close to the end. All the same, we still had to wait four days before we saw the Americans coming in. In the meantime, I'd managed to pick up a sack of potatoes, saved miraculously from the kitchen. My companions and I managed to organize it so that there was always someone sitting on the sack to protect it. This enabled us to wait for the Americans a bit more patiently.

They finally arrived one morning at around eleven. Some Americans of Italian descent were in the first tank, but I didn't understand their Sicilian accent. As it happened, there were some sons of Greek immigrants in the second armored vehicle. They told me about the thousands of dead whom they had found in the other camps they had liberated along the way. They were after the SS and killed them at the first opportunity. They left us what they had on them, chewing gum and things like that, and then they set off again.

On the following days, trucks arrived bringing us food. We were given parcels like those of the Red Cross, containing bars of chocolate, powdered milk, things that were absolutely essential, cigarettes, sugar, and wafers. But in general they hardly had time to unload the parcels. The prisoners pounced on them, grabbing as much as they could. Instead of storing them in a barrack and setting up a fair system of distribution, the Americans let themselves be completely swamped, and didn't dare intervene among us to establish order. I wanted things to be organized in a fairer way, so that the weakest, those who could barely stand upright, would get their share too. After a few days, people managed to organize themselves at least minimally. Many people died during those few days, from having eaten too much or not enough.

And what did you do to limit yourselves?

The sack of potatoes allowed us to adapt more gradually. We didn't eat them all at once, but just two or three at a time. Among the things the Americans had brought, we also found cans of pork that we mixed with the potatoes. So our stomachs didn't have to cope with anything heavy and we got used to food gradually. It also should be said that those who had been in the Sonderkommando, like myself, had arrived in the camp with more reserves. But my brother-in-law, for instance, who had been in Auschwitz for over two years, was near the end. He was already in bad shape when he came to Ebensee. Luckily, he survived. In my estimation, over half the people who had survived up to the Liberation died in the following weeks.

Did you try to take revenge?

Yes, especially on the kapos, since the Germans had fled or been captured by the Americans. The twenty-four hours that followed the Liberation gave rise to a veritable kapo-hunt. The one who had beaten me in the barrack tried to escape, but he was stopped by French prisoners. They beat him until he was almost dead. He could hardly breathe. One of the French men rose up above him. He brandished a dagger and then, turning to the others, he asked in French, "What shall we do with him? Kill him?" "KILL HIM!" the others shouted. Then he placed his knee on the kapo's chest and plunged the dagger twice into his chest. Then they took him and flung him into the pond nearby. Before throwing the body into the water, one of them wanted to take his shoes. But the man who seemed to be their leader forbade anyone to touch anything belonging to the dead man, and they threw him into the pond just as he was.

The day the Americans arrived, while the camp was thoroughly agitated, I saw, passing by, the Aryan Pole who had hit me in the face. He'd been transferred to Ebensee at the same time as I and had continued to terrorize everybody there. That day, he was wearing civilian clothes and had a bag slung over his shoulder as if he was intending to slip away. When I saw him, the blood rushed to my head. The scene in which he'd almost killed me flashed before my eyes. I seized a big stick that was lying on the ground and, with my last remaining strength, I hit him hard on the head. He tried to protect his head with his hands, as I had done when he hit me. Some watching Russians came over. I simply said to them, "kapo," and pointed at him. Without thinking, they jumped on him, grabbed his bag, and started beating him. They beat him so thoroughly that they practically killed him. He didn't experience freedom and for me that was a great source of satisfaction, since he didn't deserve any better.

After the arrival of the Americans, how long did you stay at Ebensee?

We were liberated on May 6, 1945 and I stayed until the end of June. Nearly two months, as we didn't know where to go. The French who came with the Red Cross were well organized and with great urgency took away the sickest of the French deportees. The others were repatriated to France in trucks. They were first to organize anything. The Italians did nothing. As for the Greeks, they didn't even think about doing anything.

And nobody went down into the village, as you'd predicted?

Yes, of course they did. But not to take revenge, just to find something to eat. When we were feeling a bit better, I went down with a few friends. We didn't go directly into the village, but just to the area around it, where there were a few isolated farms. As we were walking past one of these attractive farms, we saw some hens running loose. We thought we could catch one and make a nice broth that would help us recover our strength. But as soon as we went into the farmyard, the cock started to kick up a fuss. Our heads were so empty that we'd forgotten that hens don't let themselves be caught like dogs you whistle to. The hens scurried away and the cock started to get more and more aggressive. Finally I saw that one hen had stayed in the coop to lay an egg or hatch it, and so I grabbed it by the neck. The cock tried to attack me. An old Austrian opened the door of the house and shouted, *"Was ist los?"* "What's going on out there?" I replied, *"Nichts ist."* He didn't know what to do, but above all he was scared of us, so he let us make off with his hen. We killed and plucked it near the river. On the way back, we passed through the little village of Ebensee. We soon saw that the inhabitants were terrified. We only had to ask for what we wanted and they gave it us without demur. They were as scared of us as if we were wild beasts. We just asked for some beans and salt.

When we returned to the camp, we managed to find a knife to cut the chicken and a pot to cook it in. It stayed there for hours, but didn't cook properly. The smoke was terrible, and that's when I started to feel ill for the first time. I began coughing and my temperature went up. I didn't feel too sick, just weak. My health subsequently declined rapidly.

But on the first days I was still feeling quite sprightly. Three days after the arrival of the first tanks, I saw an American jeep enter the camp. The driver was alone. He climbed out of his vehicle and headed into the camp. I suppose he'd come here out of curiosity, just to see what a camp looked like. As soon as he'd gone in, I alerted some friends and we went to see what was in his jeep. Everything was there for the taking: clothes, cigarettes, anything. I lifted up the canvas covering the rear of the vehicle to see if I could find anything of interest. In the darkness, I managed to make out a crate and a few cans of stuff within arm's reach. I took everything I could, stuffing it all into my pockets. But we already had company. Many other ex-prisoners came over when they saw us. I slipped off, but when I put my hands into my pockets, I realized I'd been left with nothing. The others stole everything that I'd put into my pockets without my realizing it. I was angry and disappointed that I'd taken all that trouble for nothing. So I elbowed my way through the others to go back to the jeep. I didn't care that I was shoving them out of the way, as we'd all become savages. In the jeep, the crate was empty. I spotted one of my friends near the door. I told him in Greek to lift the lever and let down the rear door. Naturally it fell onto the heads of the people standing there. But I didn't give a damn about anything anymore; I was furious that I hadn't managed to keep anything. Inside, in a corner, I saw a big sack. Instead of helping myself to some of its contents, I preferred to take the whole thing to avoid the same mishap. Everyone pounced on me and tried to steal the sack. I told my brother-in-law and my friends to hit out at the others and push them away so we could keep the sack for ourselves. Finally, we managed to get it safely back to the little barrack that the SS had used at the entrance of the camp.

My friends immediately tried to open the sack to see what was inside. But I told them to wait, since I wanted to see how the soldier was going to react. I heard him coming back, whistling to himself. When he saw his jeep and all the prisoners gathered round it, he pulled out his pistol and fired two shots into the air to send everyone away. Then he merely raised the rear door and drove away. Only then did I open the sack. Inside, there were several packs of cigarettes – Camel, Lucky Strike, and some others, as well as some matches. I took out one cigarette and passed it around to everyone, as if it were a marvelous treasure. Then I lit it, but it was much too strong compared to the handmade fags I was used to. I started to cough, I felt dizzy because of the tobacco and the illness to which I was gradually succumbing. In the sack, we also found some towels, a handsome cap, and two cameras. We shared out the booty among us. The problem lay in finding a safe hiding-place for all of it. The cigarettes were hidden under a mattress, but it was impossible for someone to sit there all the time to protect them.

Actually, they were stolen from me shortly afterwards. I knew that Salvatore Cunio (the Greek who had acted as an interpreter on our arrival in Auschwitz – he spoke English as well as German) had been sent to the rail station to supervise a group of Austrians whom the Americans had set to work to clean up the station. These Austrian civilians were doing the same work they had forced us to do. But now they were under the supervision of ex-prisoners who stood guard over them. The recently liberated were happy to be able to savor a bit of revenge in this way – but of course, all this happened under the overall control of the Americans. So I went along, curious to see for myself. But I'd have done better not to get out of bed on that day. When I came back, someone had stolen all my cigarettes, as well as the two cameras that I'd left in the sack. I went to the bed of a sick man who never left his bunk, opposite mine. I asked him who'd come and stolen my cigarettes. He pretended he hadn't seen anything, but I merely had to raise my voice and he admitted that he had stolen my things. I got my cigarettes back without difficulty, but not the cameras, which he claimed he'd thrown into the lake.

Did you still have enough strength for a convincing show of force?

Yes. Even though I already was very ill, I still didn't realize this. I discovered it only when the Americans decided to transfer us to a military camp they had set up for that purpose. The place we were in was actually quite filthy and the Americans realized they'd have to disinfect everything to avoid risks of an epidemic. So that we wouldn't contaminate the new place on arrival, the Americans made us take a shower, spraying us with DDT to eliminate lice. Then we had to be X-rayed. If the doctors spotted anything abnormal, they set us to one side so we could be treated. I was X-rayed and they told me step to one side, but they didn't say why. They examined me a second time, before confirming that something was wrong with my lungs. They immediately took me to the tent that served as a hospital. The beds were comfortable, the white sheets immac-

ulate. For me, it was like sleeping in a palace. But I stayed
there for just a few days, because I didn't feel ill, and I wanted
to go back to my friends. When I found out they intended to
go to Eretz Yisrael, to Palestine, I left the hospital – I wanted
to go with them. There was nowhere else for me to go, and
nobody with whom to be reunited. I didn't want to stay all by
myself, with nobody at all.

Did you know exactly what kind of illness you had?

I found out when a friend came to see me. He picked up my
medical notes and read "TB." I didn't know what that was. He
explained it to me: "Tuberculosis – it means you've got a lung
disease." I wasn't worried; I was sure that with the food and
the medicine they were giving me, I'd soon be cured.

So, two or three days later, I declared that I wanted to leave
and I joined up with my friends, who were heading for
Palestine via Italy. The Americans handed us over to some
British people and so we set off, five or six truck-loads of us.
That's when I started to feel really ill. I was in great pain. The
truck dropped me and other patients off at a hospital in Udine,
in the north of Italy. I was filled with anguish at the idea that
my friends were going to leave for Palestine without me. An
agent of the Haganah[1] came to see me in the hospital to assure
me that I'd be able to go too, as soon as my health allowed. So
I stayed with the other patients, all of whom came, like me,
from the camp at Ebensee.

Later on, I was sent to the sanatorium at Forlanini. I
was the only ex-deportee there, together with several other
tuberculosis sufferers. I stayed there from July 1945 until

---

[1] A clandestine defense organization in Palestine during the British man-
date, fighting to defend the Jews and establish the State of Israel. Immediately after the war, the Haganah helped many survivors of the Shoah to
emigrate to Palestine.

November 1946 and made some good friends. I was the only
one who didn't get any visits from my family, but everyone
shared with me the things that were brought. There, the men's
hospital was opposite the women's hospital. When we talked
to each other through the windows, the girls called me *bruno,*
the one with brown hair. This name stuck and all of them got
to know me by that name. I didn't want to reassume my old
first name, in case it all started again. So, instead of Shlomo or
Solomon, my official first name, I became "Bruno."

Did you tell them what you'd endured in the camps?

No, absolutely nothing, not to anyone. For a long time,
nobody knew that I was Jewish. Nobody asked me, since they
barely even suspected the existence of the camps. I was the
only Jew in that hospital. After some time, I was contacted by
a young Jewish woman from the DELASEM.[2] Her name was
Bianca Pinkerle and she went round the hospitals asking
whether there were any people there who were on their own,
without families. She lived in Trieste, but she traveled the distance every fortnight to visit me.

One day, she asked me whether by any chance I knew a certain Niccolò Sagi, who had also been deported to Auschwitz.
I told her I didn't know people's names, but I might be able to
recognize faces. The next time, she brought a photo. I recognized the man straightaway: he was particularly tall and red-
haired (I could tell as much even though when I knew him his
head was shaved). I'd seen him in the Sonderkommando and
I knew he'd been killed during the revolt. She told me that
he'd been deported with his son Luigi. She wanted to gather
as much information as possible to transmit it to the wife of

[2] The DELASEM (Delegazione Assistenza degli Emigranti Ebrei/
Delegation for the Assistance of Jewish Emigrants) was the main Jewish
Italian organization for giving aid to survivors of the Shoah.

this Niccolò Sagi, who was waiting for him in Trieste. Years later, Luigi Sagi became one of my best friends.

In November 1946, Bianca suggested that I be transferred to a hospital in Merano, an institution run by the American Jewish Joint Distribution Committee.[3] She went with me by ambulance to Florence, then I continued on to Merano. I stayed in that hospital for several years. As well as providing treatment, the "Joint" helped patients to be re-integrated into professional life. They paid for a house that we shared with two or three other people, so we could learn gradually to get back into active life. With an instructor who'd come from Venice with the express purpose of giving us lessons, I learned to work in leather. Very few of the patients survived their illness. Subsequently, the Joint decided to shut down the Merano hospital since several patients had decided to emigrate to Israel, Canada, or the United States, thanks again to that organization. Those who stayed were sent to Grottaferrata, near Rome, where we were given a house and other assistance. They gave us some money every month, which meant that I could take English lessons and, later on, lessons at the hotel-management school on Lake Como, with my friend Luigi Sagi.

All in all, I spent seven years, after my liberation from the camps, in various hospitals. I lost the use of one lung, but the care I was given every day, following different treatments, finally led to my recovery.

How did you meet your wife?

I met her in the English classes I was taking in Grottaferrata. Marika was only just seventeen, I was thirty-two. Her father

---

[3] The American Jewish Joint Distribution Committee (JDC) was created in 1914 to provide aid to needy Jews throughout the world.

had fled from Hungary during the war, which she had spent in Nice with her grandmother. Then, when she came to live near Rome, we met. She came to join me when I started working in a hotel in Rimini and we got married. I was lucky, since it wasn't easy to find a woman like her – one who could put up with my personality. We had three sons together: Mario, Alessandro, and Alberto.

When did you first hear about your brother and sister after the Liberation?

I received news about my brother while I was still in the Ebensee camp, after the Liberation. The men who could still walk went to other camps to see if they could get any news about their friends and family. One day I met a Greek friend, David Tabò, who was in the same camp as my brother. He told me that my brother was ill, but still alive. I later found out that he had been in a coma when the Liberation occurred. He came out of his coma three months later, in a good hospital. He didn't know what had happened, or where he was. I received letters from him while I was in the hospital at Udine. Then I saw him again, seven years after the Liberation. He was traveling through Italy to emigrate to the United States. I went to meet him at the port, we spent a few hours together, and then he left. I saw my sister again in Israel in 1957. She had picked up my trail at the hospital, thanks to my brother-in-law, Aaron Mano, whom she had married before going to live in Israel.

Of all our family, only three of us survived. That's already a miracle, when you think of all the families who were completely wiped out, from which no one is left to preserve any memories. For example, my mother's brothers, with their wives and children. . . . Nobody came back. The family name of their branch, "Angel," died out with them.

What were their names?

My mother's elder brother was Avraham Angel; I don't remember his wife's first name, but I know that his two sons were called Sylvain and Haïm. I even still have a photo of Sylvain when he was about ten, posing with a cigarette in his hand, as they did in those days. Then came Haïm, who was married but didn't have any children. Then Meïr, who also was married and without children. The youngest of my uncles was called Sabbetaï; he had two daughters, but unfortunately I've forgotten their names.

When did you start to tell the story of what you had seen and experienced in Birkenau?

I started to talk about it very belatedly, since people didn't want to listen, they didn't want to believe it had happened. It wasn't that I was unwilling to talk. When I came out of the hospital, I found myself in the company of a Jewish man and I started to talk. All of a sudden, I realized that, instead of looking at me, he was looking behind me at someone who was making signs to him. I turned around and was surprised to catch one of his friends gesturing that I was completely mad. I shut up and from that time on I didn't want to talk about it anymore. For me, it was painful to talk, so when I came across people who didn't believe me, I told myself there was no point.

It was only in 1992, forty-seven years after my liberation, that I started to talk again. The problem of anti-Semitism was resurfacing in Italy. You saw more and more swastikas scribbled onto the walls. . . . I returned to Auschwitz for the first time in December 1992. I'd hesitated for a long time before going along with the school that had invited me, since I didn't feel ready to go back to hell. My friend Luigi Sagi went with me. I didn't know that the Nazis had blown up the crematoria when they left, so I was surprised to see the ruins. I returned several times the following years. But the Polish guides made me furious: they didn't take all the groups to Birkenau and presented history as if everything had happened in Auschwitz I.

These days, do you feel the need to bear witness?

When I feel well, yes. But it's difficult. And I'm a meticulous person, who likes things to be clear and done properly. When I go to tell my story in a school and the teacher hasn't prepared the pupils properly, I feel deeply wounded. Once I've happened to be in a classroom before the lady teacher arrived and a kid came to ask me what we were going to talk about. But, overall, bearing witness in schools gives me considerable satisfaction. I sometimes receive very moving letters from people who were touched by the story I told.

It comforts me to know that I'm not talking in a vacuum, since bearing witness exacts a huge sacrifice. It reawakens a nagging pain that never leaves me. Everything's going fine and then, all of a sudden, I'm in despair. As soon as I feel a little joy, something inside me closes up immediately. It's like an inner flaw; I call it "the survivors' disease." It's not typhus, tuberculosis, or the other diseases that people sometimes caught. It's a disease that gnaws away at us from within and destroys any feeling of joy. I have been dragging it about with me ever since I spent that time suffering in the camp. This disease never leaves me a moment of joy or carefree happiness; it's a mood that forever erodes my strength.

Do you think that there is any difference between you, as a survivor of the Sonderkommando, and the other survivors from Auschwitz?

Yes, I think so, even if I know that saying so hurts some people's feelings. The other survivors certainly suffered from cold and hunger more than I did, but they weren't constantly in contact with the dead. This vision, day after day, of all those victims who had been gassed. . . . The fact of seeing all those groups arriving and entering without hope, having lost all joy. They were all at the end of their strength; it was really terrible to see. If I say that the experience of being in the Sonderkommando weighed much more heavily, this was because I had occasion, in Melk and Ebensee, to share the common experience of other deportees.

Have you talked about all of this to your wife and children?

No, absolutely not. It wouldn't have done me any good to talk to them about it. On the contrary, it would have inflicted on them a weight that was useless, and difficult to bear. Only recently did they start to discover my story. I did all I could to avoid them being marked by it. But I know that I couldn't behave like a normal father who helps his children to do their homework and merrily plays with them. I was lucky to have a very intelligent wife who was able to manage that side of things.

What was destroyed in you by that extreme experience?

Life. Since then I've never had a normal life. I've never been able to pretend that everything was all right and go off dancing, like others, without a care in the world. . . .

Everything takes me back to the camp. Whatever I do, whatever I see, my mind keeps harking back to the same place. It's as if the "work" I was forced to do there had never really left my head. . . .

Nobody ever really gets out of the Crematorium.

HISTORICAL NOTES

THE SHOAH, AUSCHWITZ, AND THE SONDERKOMMANDO

by Marcello Pezzetti

The process of persecution of the Jews occurred in three phases:

1. from 1933 to 1939 ("The Jews in the Reich: From Discrimination to Emigration");
2. from 1939 to 1941 ("The War: From Ghettoization to the Formulation of the 'Final Solution' (*Endlösung*)");
3. from 1941 to 1945 ("Mass Extermination: The Shoah").

THE JEWS IN THE REICH: FROM DISCRIMINATION TO EMIGRATION (1933–1939)

The first phase concerned almost exclusively the Jews within the German Reich.[1] During this period, Nazi policies aimed

---

[1] For a detailed analysis of the period, see Wolfgang Benz (ed.), *Die Juden in Deutschland 1933–1945: Leben unter nationalsozialistischer Herrschaft* (Munich: Beck, 1966), Saul Friedländer, *Nazi Germany and the Jews*, vol. I, *The Years of Persecution 1933–1939* (New York: HarperCollins, 1997), and Raul Hilberg, *The Destruction of the European Jews*, Third Edition (New Haven: Yale University Press, 2003).

at the objective of Jewish emigration, thereby manifesting the first enactment of anti-Semitism that hitherto had been simply the expression of a political ideology. Hitler, constrained by the pressure of international opinion and a certain proportion of German opinion, proceeded stage by stage in this first period. The beginning, on April 1, 1933, of the first campaign boycotting Jewish shops (an action which aroused no more than a muffled reaction in the German population and an equally muted reaction abroad) constituted the first real attack on the domestic national Jewish community via the professional sphere.

On April 7, 1933, the "Law on the Restoration of the Civil Service" for the first time provided a juridical definition of "non-Aryan," whereby it was enough for a single one of the grandparents not to be Aryan for an individual to be defined as "non-Aryan." This definition, known as the "*Arierparagraph,*" constituted the point of departure for all successive persecutions meted out to Jews and also to Roma and Sinti (Gypsies).

On the basis of this law, several arrangements targeted the various social and professional categories within the German Jewish community, beginning with jurists and doctors, then teachers and university professors, and including even the sectors of agriculture, journalism, and indeed sport (such as the aryanization of sports complexes, decreed on May 24, 1933).

After a period of relative calm, a new and violent campaign of anti-Jewish propaganda was launched in 1935. Its culminating point was the promulgation of the "Law for the Defense of German Blood and Honor" and the "Law on Reich Citizenship," better known as the "Nuremberg Laws." These laws categorized the Jews as "purely Jewish," "first-degree mixed" (*Mischlinge),* and "second-degree mixed." For the first time in history, these measures imposed the isolation of Jews from the rest of the population on the basis of biological factors. The consequences of this decision led to the exclusion of

Jews from all forms of social life. From November 14, 1935, Jews were stripped of their civil rights (notably the right to vote). Civil servants, university professors, teachers, doctors, and lawyers, who had until then been able to take advantage of exceptional dispensations, were all dismissed. Mixed marriages and marriages between "*Mischlinge*" were forbidden. Any sexual relationships between Jews and Aryans were considered as "a race crime" (*Rassenschande*); this was the most fundamental indication of anti-Semitism. Approximately 502,000 Jews considered "pure" (i.e., completely Jewish), and 250,000 persons considered as "*Mischlinge*," were affected by these laws.

In the first phase (1933–39), 1938 turned out to be a decisive year. On April 26, the Jews were ordered to declare all their belongings, which marked the beginning of the process of the systematic "aryanization" of Jewish businesses and struck a profound blow against those who were seeking to emigrate. March 1938 marked the time of the "*Anschluss*" (the "annexation" of Austria to the territory of the Reich). All the anti-Jewish measures promulgated in Germany over the first six years of the regime were automatically applied to Austria. That country thus became a testing ground for adapting, in occupied countries, the anti-Semitic policies decreed by the Nazi regime. This year also saw the failure of various international bodies to find a "solution" to the problem of refugees, mainly Jews. Apart from the patent failure of the League of Nations, the Evian Conference, organized in July to solve the question, failed lamentably because no country, not even the United States, declared itself ready to welcome in threatened Jews. The existing quotas were rigorously enforced.[2]

[2] The Evian Conference, in which thirty-two countries took part, was held between July 6 and 15, 1938. On July 13 the Nazi Party newspaper, the *Völkischer Beobachter*, ran a triumphant headline saying (of the Jews) "Nobody Wants Them."

On November 9, the *"Pogromnacht"* (generally called "Reichskristallnacht") occurred;[3] this marked the end of spontaneous anti-Semitic acts and reassured the bureaucrats that the German people as a whole were indifferent to the anti-Jewish policies of the regime. The pogrom was rapidly followed by a new wave of mass arrests.

The fact that Jews were imprisoned in *Lager* was not in itself new; but hitherto, this had not been a mass phenomenon. So this was the first time that Jews as such, simply because they were Jewish, were included within the system of the "concentration camps."

This "system" had been operating since spring 1933, when, after the burning of the Reichstag, the regime adopted a series of preventive measures targeting the expression of any form of political opposition. The people arrested (Communists, pacifists, Social Democrats, trade union members, Jews active in workers' organizations, and certain non-aligned churchmen) were imprisoned as a measure of "protective detention" (*Schutzhaft*)[4] in a number of camps, among which the most infamous was Dachau. The prisoners were subjected to particularly difficult conditions of detention characterized by violence, arbitrary torture, and, in some cases, executions. However, the length of time for which they were detained and the conditions in which they were kept could vary, and several prisoners were released after a few months of imprisonment.[5] In 1934, Heinrich Himmler, *Reichsführer* of the SS, managed

---

[3] Ninety-one people were killed during this pogrom, 191 synagogues were destroyed and 7,500 shops ransacked.

[4] Gudrun Schwarz, *Die nationalsozialistischen Lager* (Frankfurt-am-Main and New York: Campus, 1990), pp. 21–33.

[5] For a detailed analysis of this first phase of the concentration camp system, see Klaus Drobish and Günther Wieland, *System der NS-Konzentrationslager 1933–1939* (Berlin: Akademie Verlag, 1993); Johannes Tuchel, *Konzentrationslager: Organisationsgeschichte und Funktion der "Inspektion der Konzentrationslager" 1934–1938* (Boppard: H. Boldt, 1991).

to bring all the camps under his total control and to embark on a broad process of reorganization of the Nazi concentration camp system.[6]

Between 1936 and 1937, developments within this system rested on two main factors. On the one side, there was the realization of the four-year plan defined by Hermann Göring, whose main objective was German rearmament (in principle forbidden by the Versailles Treaty). In anticipation of an approaching war, the plan provided for the use of the prison workforce in factories run by the SS.[7] The other decisive factor was the extension of the principle of "protective detention" to other social categories defined more broadly to include all persons considered "harmful" to the *"Volksgemeinschaft"* (the "community of the people"): common law criminals, the work-shy, persons infected by contagious diseases (especially VD), prostitutes, homosexuals, vagrants, alcoholics, psychopaths, and disturbers of public order (including dangerous drivers), as well as possibly some nightclub and cabaret performers and professional dancers, all of them considered as "asocial" or antisocial, as were Jehovah's Witnesses and Roma and Sinti (Gypsies), who were deemed "parasites on the nation" (*"Volksschädlinge"*).[8]

From 1936 onwards, five large KL (*Konzentrationslager*) were opened to intern these new categories and the regime's opponents: Sachsenhausen (1936), Buchenwald (1937), Flossenbürg (1938), Mauthausen (1938, after the *"Anschluss"*),

[6] Norbert Frei, *Der Führerstaat: Nationalsozialistische Herrschaft 1933 bis 1945* (Munich: Deutscher Taschenbuch Verlag, 2002), p. 139.

[7] Dieter Pohl, *Verfolgung und Massenmord in der NS-Zeit 1933–1945* (Darmstadt: Wissenschaftliche Buchgesellschaft, 2003), p. 140.

[8] Ulrich Herbert, "Von der Gegnerbekämpfung zur 'rassischen Generalprävention,'" in Ulrich Herbert, Karin Orth, and Christoph Dieckmann, *Die nationalsozialistischen Konzentrationslager: Entwicklung und Struktur* (Frankfurt-am-Main: Fischer Taschenbuch Verlag, 2002), pp. 78–80.

and Ravensbrück (1939, a women's camp).[9] The increase in the population of the concentration camps led to the adoption of a system to designate various categories by different-colored triangles: red for political prisoners, black for the "asocial," brown for Gypsies, purple for Jehovah's Witnesses (*Bibelforscher*), pink for homosexuals, green for common law criminals, blue for the stateless, and two crossed triangles, one of them yellow, for Jews. Throughout this phase, the death rate increased suddenly, reaching 5 percent in Dachau and over 9 percent in Buchenwald.[10] This rate continued to increase. On the eve of the war, the death rate at Buchenwald reached nearly 14 percent.

It is important to emphasize that the Jews were not, before 1938, included systematically in this repressive penal system. The large numbers of them who, from 1933 onwards, were sent to the camps within the concentration camp system were sent generally because they belonged to another "category" of persons targeted by legislation

When, from November 9, 1938, the round-ups started to affect the Jewish population as a whole, approximately 35,000 persons were imprisoned, mainly in the camps at Buchenwald, Sachsenhausen, and Dachau. In less than three months, 243 of them were killed, more than over the previous five years.[11] But the majority of them were freed, after having declared that they would emigrate.

---

[9] Karin Orth, *Die Konzentrationslager-SS: Sozialstrukturelle Analysen und biographische Studien* (Munich: Deutscher Taschenbuch Verlag, 2004), pp. 24–5.

[10] Walter Bartel and Klaus Trostorff (eds), *Buchenwald: Mahnung und Verpflichtung* (East Berlin: VEB Deutscher Verlag der Wissenschaften (DDR), 1983), p. 698.

[11] Stanislav Zámečnik, *C'était ça, Dachau. 1933–1945* (Paris: Le cherche midi, 2003), pp. 113–14.

THE WAR: FROM GHETTOIZATION TO THE FORMULATION OF THE "FINAL SOLUTION" (1939–1941)

The period from 1939 to 1941, characterized by the outbreak of the worldwide conflict, represented the second phase in the process of persecution and destruction of the Jews of Europe. On September 1, 1939, German troops invaded Polish territory. It was in this country of 27,000,000 inhabitants that the largest Jewish community in Central and Eastern Europe was found, comprising over 3,200,000 persons. So the Jews constituted nearly 12 percent of the total population and over 30 percent of the urban population.

Seventeen days after the outbreak of war, Poland was divided between the two invading powers, Germany and the Soviet Union. The Jewish population, more numerous in the part under German control, was thus subjected to the anti-Jewish policies of the Nazi regime. A major demographic restructuring of the territory was undertaken; it consisted of "repatriating" the *Volksdeutsche* (persons of German ethnic origin) who lived in Soviet territory, and expelling the local populations who were deemed dangerous from a "racial" point of view (mainly Jews, but also certain Poles considered "non-germanizable").[12] It was a question of shifting the Reich's "ethnic" frontier over five hundred miles. This plan thus created the conditions to make the Reich *"judenfrei"* (free of Jews), via the forced emigration eastwards of the whole Jewish population of the Reich.

In the two months that followed the invasion, the territories occupied by Germany were divided into two distinct

---

[12] For further details on this subject, see Peter Longerich, *Politik der Vernichtung: Eine Gesamtdarstellung der nazionalsozialistischen Judenverfolgung* (Munich and Zurich: Piper, 1998), and Götz Aly, *"Endlösung": Völkerverschiebung und der Mord an den europäischen Juden* (Frankfurt-am-Main: Fischer Verlag, 1998).

parts: the territories in the west of Poland (Upper Silesia, the Warthegau, the district of Danzig-Pomerania, and East Prussia) were incorporated into the Reich, while those in central and east Poland (the districts of Lublin, Kraków, Radom, and Warsaw) were transformed into a reserve for a labor force. That territory was called the "General Government," and placed under rigid German administration.

Special SS troops were used to eliminate part of the Polish elite, as well as many Jews, so as to expel them as quickly as possible. In addition, new KL were set up in the conquered territories to imprison the local intelligentsia and a new category of prisoners: prisoners of war. Thus, from September 2 onwards, KL-Stutthof was opened near Danzig,[13] and in April 1940, KL-Auschwitz was set up between Kraków and Katowice.

To facilitate the expulsion eastwards of the whole of the Jewish population, a plan was drawn up to bring together and concentrate the Jewish population into urban centers. From spring 1940 onwards began the systematic ghettoization of the Polish Jews (including, in certain cases, as in Łódź , part of the Gypsy population). In certain places, such as Piotrków Tribunalski, this operation took place as early as October 1939, while in certain other towns, such as Białystok, sealing off the ghetto was postponed until September 1941. The first major operation took place in the annexed region of the Warthegau (providing a blueprint for all successive operations), with the establishment of the Łódź ghetto in the most dilapidated part of town. At the beginning of February, the Chief of Police promulgated an order establishing a *Jüdischer Wohnbezirk* (a Jewish dwelling zone); on March 8, the Nazis massacred nearly 2,000 Jews found outside the designated

---

[13] Mirosław Gliński, "Organisation und Struktur des Lagers Stutthof," in Donald Stayer (ed.), *Stutthof: Das Konzentrationslager* (Gdańsk: Wydawnictwo "Marpress," 1996), p. 77.

district; on May 1 the ghetto was hermetically sealed and an order announced the execution of any Jew found outside the ghetto; finally, the possessions that the victims had been forced to abandon behind them were systematically pillaged.

Town by town, the local administrations adopted the same procedure, with a few adaptations, in particular when it came to the assembling of small dispersed Jewish communities into towns that became town-ghettos (such as the small town of Szydłowiec) or in Kraków, where the process of ghettoization followed a different pattern.[14]

The ghetto was generally formed of a set of buildings without any open or green spaces, situated in the center of the town and next to a railway station (according to Reinhard Heydrich's instructions). In some cities such as Warsaw (the most populous ghetto, in which 450,000 Jews were confined), Kraków, or Radom, a wall (reminiscent of medieval city walls with entry gates) was built around the ghetto. In other cities, such as Łódź, only barbed-wire fences surrounded the ghetto, and in yet other cities, such as Lublin, there was no wall or fence.[15]

In tandem with this, a set of labor camps, the *Zwangsarbeitslager* or ZAL, designed to exploit the Jewish workforce, were established across the territory.

However, as far as Nazi policies were concerned, the ghettos could represent only a temporary solution to a much wider territorial problem. Between spring 1940 and summer 1941, with the waves of expulsion of Jews from West to East and the

[14] In Kraków, Governor Hans Frank proceeded to a drastic reduction of the Jewish population in the city even before the establishment of the ghetto on March 3, 1941. The Jewish population of some 70,000 persons in 1939 was forced into emigration. In October 1941 the number of those expelled had already reached 32,000 persons.

[15] On the Warsaw ghetto, see Israel Gutman, *Resistance: The Warsaw Ghetto Uprising* (New York: Houghton Mifflin Company in association with the United States Holocaust Memorial Museum, 1994).

gathering of local Jews, the Nazi bureaucracy progressively transformed the program of forced emigration into a policy for the "*Endlösung der Judenfrage*" (final solution of the Jewish question).

MASS EXTERMINATION: THE SHOAH (1941–1945)

The third phase was that of physical extermination. It began in June 1941 with the invasion of the Soviet Union.

The invasion forces were followed by "special troops"[16] (*Einsatzgruppen*), whose task it was to shoot the Jewish population within the field of intervention (which spread progressively from the Baltic to all of White Russia). These "mobile combat units" of the SS managed to carry out their destructive task with the help of the Wehrmacht and elements recruited among the local population, some of whom joined the auxiliary troops of the SS. The number of their victims is estimated at between 1,500,000 and 1,800,000 persons.[17]

In order to eliminate the Jews on Soviet territory, the Germans used the method of mass execution that seemed to them, in this case, to be the most efficient way of achieving the desired aim. This system of murder, adopted by mobile units, allowed them to eliminate the greatest number of possible victims who had not been forced to live, as in Poland, in lim-

---

[16] Cf. Helmut Krausnick, *Hitlers Einsatzgruppen: Die Truppen des Weltanschauungskrieges 1938–1942* (Frankfurt-am-Main: Fischer Taschenbuch Verlag, 1993), and Peter Klein (ed.), *Die Einsatzgruppen in der besetzten Sowjetunion 1941/42: Die Tätigkeits- und Lageberichte des Chefs der Sicherheitspolizei und des SD* (Berlin: Edition Hentrich, 1997).

[17] Research undertaken by Father Patrick Desbois should show a considerable increase in the number of victims of the Einsatzgruppen. See his *The Holocaust by Bullets* (New York: Palgrave Macmillan, 2008). Also see Joshua Rubenstein and Ilya Altman (eds), *The Unknown Black Book: The Holocaust in the German-Occupied Soviet Territories* (Bloomington: Indiana University Press in association with the United States Holocaust Memorial Museum, 2008).

ited urban centers. But major problems rapidly cropped up and forced the German bureaucracy to identify new methods of murder, establishing a more "distant" relation between the victims and their executioners. In addition, the presence of gigantic common graves near the big cities and the fact that it was practically impossible to hide from local populations the reality of these mass executions, and, as a result, not attract attention from international public opinion, made the situation almost untenable. In a short time, the psychological state of some of the troops carrying out the massacres became a matter of concern to various echelons of the leadership.

Mass executions were not the only method of murder practiced by the regime. Indeed, after the outbreak of the war, a vast secret plan was developed inside the Reich with the aim of preserving the purity of the "*Volksgemeinschaft.*" This plan, with the name *Aktion T4*, involved the elimination of the mentally ill. It began with the death of handicapped children by injecting them with fatal doses of medicine. Then, another technique was developed to bring about death in adults: gassing by inhalation of pure carbon monoxide, from a canister, in institutes specially furnished for this purpose and provided with gas chambers. This operation cost the lives of approximately 70,000–80,000 victims.[18] The technique was repeated and used again between 1939 and 1940 in asylums and sanatoria in Poland, Pomerania, and East Prussia, to eliminate interned

---

[18] *Aktion T4* was suspended in summer 1941, mainly because of public disapproval and the commitment shown by Church leaders to ensuring that these operations ceased. A number of the state functionaries who contributed to *Aktion T4* were sent to work in the different KL, organizing the executions of prisoners judged to be incapable of work (an operation designated by the code name "14f13"). Cf. Henry Friedlander, *The Origins of Nazi Genocide: From Euthanasia to the Final Solution* (Chapel Hill and London: University of North Carolina Press, 1995), and Ernst Klee (ed.), *Dokumente zur "Euthanasie"* (Frankfurt-am-Main: Fischer Verlag, 2001).

patients. There, the gas was inhaled from canisters of carbon monoxide installed in the trucks transporting the victims.

Between summer and autumn 1941, the Nazi bureaucracy took the decision to use these methods of programmed and scientific "elimination" on the Jewish population of occupied Europe. This was the biggest murder project ever conceived. To this end, the administration needed to define the operational methods that would be the most effective in achieving this large-scale goal.

In September, experiments in fixed-place gas chambers resumed, in the region of Minsk.[19] However, there was a new element as compared with the method used in operation T4: the gas used was the exhaust gas from the engine, introduced into the chamber by pipes. At the same time, a variant of the *Gaswagen* (gas trucks) was tested in Ukraine with the gas being fed in no longer by canisters but directly via the exhaust pipe.[20] The Gaswagen were adopted for the first big murder operation carried out in December, in Chełmno, on Jews from the Łódź ghetto and the zones around the Wartheland. The same types of vehicles were used at almost the same time in Serbia, in the Semlin camp, to kill the Jews of Belgrade.

The systematic elimination of the Jews of the General Government (also including East Galicia, after the invasion of the USSR) was organized between the end of 1941 and the beginning of 1942. The operation, which was subsequently called "*Aktion Reinhard*," was entrusted to the chief of police of the Lublin district, Odilo Globocnik, and his collaborator, Christian Wirth. The latter, as did many civil servants who

---

[19] Cf. Michael Tregenza, *Purificare e distruggere: (1) Il programma "Eutanasia." Le prime camere a gas naziste e lo sterminio dei disabili (1939–1941)* (Verona: Ombre Corte, 2006), pp. 111–17.

[20] Cf. Mathias Beer, "Die Entwicklung der Gaswagen beim Mord an den Juden," *Vierteljahrshefte für Zeitgeschichte*, vol. 35, no. 3 (1987), pp. 403–17.

went on to work on the elimination of the Jews of the General Government, had been directly involved in implementing operation T4.

In order to carry out this task, three places were identified as having good rail links and thus suitable for building murder installations, fixed-site gas chambers with motor gas pumped in: Bełzec (between Kraków and Lwów), Sobibór (near Lublin) and Treblinka (between Warsaw and Białystok). The first camp to function was Bełzec, in March 1942, then Sobibór between April and May, and finally Treblinka in July.[21]

The three camps were constructed on an identical basic composite structure: a sector reserved for the dwelling blocks for the guards (mainly Ukrainians) and a very limited number of prisoners who picked up and sorted possessions stolen from the victims (in Bełzec, the first camp to be opened, this distinction was not as rigid); a sector around the ramp inside the camp for the "unloading" of the Jews (the tracks running right into the camp); a zone of barracks for storing the objects (*Sortierplatz*); a space and a building in which the victims had to undress; an obligatory zone of passage for the victims (*Schlauch* – a tube) surrounded by barbed wire; a building at the end of this *Schlauch* in which the gas chambers were located, plus a room with a big diesel motor; and finally a large open space for the common graves in which the bodies were at first buried, and subsequently burned in the open.

In 1943, after the liquidation of almost all the Polish ghettos and the setting up of the new structures of extermination in Birkenau (including gas chambers and crematorium ovens), *Aktion Reinhard* came to an end and the structures were

---

[21] For further details on this theme, see Hilberg, *The Destruction of the European Jews*, Yitzhak Arad, *Belzec, Sobibor, Treblinka: The Operation Reinhard Death Camps* (Bloomington: Indiana University Press, 1987), and Dieter Pohl, *Von der "Judenpolitik" zum Judenmord: Der Distrikt Lublin des Generalgouvernements 1939–1944* (Frankfurt-am-Main: Peter Lang, 1993).

definitively dismantled in autumn. This operation killed over 1,700,000 victims in these three camps, in addition to all the Jews killed during the liquidation of the various ghettos, as well as those who were killed in the forced labor camps for Jews inside the General Government.

AUSCHWITZ-BIRKENAU AND ITS ROLE IN THE "FINAL SOLUTION"

On April 27, 1940, KL-Auschwitz was established in a former military barracks in the small town of Oświęcim situated in the territory of Eastern Upper Silesia that had shortly before been annexed to the Reich. It was initially created as a concentration camp for Polish political opponents.[22] On May 4, 1940, SS-Hauptsturmführer Rudolf Höß (who came from KL-Sachsenhausen) was appointed camp commandant. As in all the Nazi KL, a crematorium (*Krematorium I*) was installed as a sanitary measure so as to burn the corpses and thus avoid the spread of epidemics. The crematorium at Auschwitz was thus built and delivered by the German firm Topf & Söhne, of Erfurt.[23]

During his first visit to the camp on March 1, 1941, Himmler gave orders to extend the *Lager* in view of the imminent arrival of 30,000 prisoners and to place at the dis-

---

[22] On the history of the Auschwitz camp, see Yisrael Gutman and Michael Berenbaum (eds), *Anatomy of the Auschwitz Death Camp* (Bloomington: Indiana University Press in association with the United States Holocaust Memorial Museum, 1994); Sybille Steinbacher, *"Musterstadt" Auschwitz: Germanisierungspolitik und Judenmord in Ostoberschlesien* (Munich: Saur, 2000); Danuta Czech, *Kalendarium der Ereignisse im Konzentrationslager Auschwitz-Birkenau 1939–1945* (Reinbek bei Hamburg: Rowohlt, 1989); and Wacław Długoborski and Franciszek Piper (eds), *Studien zur Geschichte des Konzentrations- und Vernichtungslagers Auschwitz*, 5 vols (Oświęcim: Verlag des Staatlichen Museums Auschwitz-Birkenau, 1999).

[23] For further details on the structure of the crematoria, see Jean-Claude Pressac, *Auschwitz: Technique and Operation of the Gas Chambers* (New York: The Beate Klarsfeld Foundation, 1989), and his *Les Crématoires d'Auschwitz: La machinerie du meurtre de masse* (Paris: CNRS Éditions, 1993).

posal of the largest German chemical company, IG Farben, 10,000 prisoners who would be building the firm's new factory in the neighboring village of Dwory.

Between summer and autumn of the same year, the Auschwitz administration carried out experiments on new murder techniques similar to those that were being tried in the East. At the beginning of September, 600 Soviet prisoners of war and 250 Polish prisoners who were sick and deemed unsuitable for work were sent to a room in the basement of Block 11 and killed with Zyklon B gas. This gas had hitherto been used solely to disinfect barracks and clothing. Following this first experiment in mass gassing with Zyklon B, part of the mortuary room of Crematorium I was transformed into a gas chamber. It was in this "provisional" gas chamber that Soviet prisoners of war were eliminated, as were prisoners deemed unsuitable for work (within the context of "*Aktion 14f13*") and the first transports of Jews from Upper Silesia.

At the end of September 1941, the order was given to build a huge new camp some two miles away from the *Stammlager* (main camp). This order gave rise to the camp at Birkenau (later called Auschwitz II-Birkenau), initially planned as a camp for prisoners of war (*KGL – Kriegsgefangenenlager*), principally Soviet POWs. But within two months, the decision was taken in Berlin, at the instigation of the big industries, to make large-scale use of the Soviet labor force within the Reich. This was decisive for the future of Birkenau, since the camp, although built by and for Russian prisoners, eventually became a mainly Jewish prison. This change in direction was confirmed by an order from Himmler dated January 25, 1942, announcing that Jews rather than Soviet POWs would be sent there.[24]

---

[24] From October 7, 1941, the first large groups of Soviet prisoners began to arrive in Auschwitz. In barely a month, nearly 10,000 Soviet prisoners

At the Wannsee conference, at the beginning of 1942, plans for the elimination of all the Jews of Europe were presented to the leaders of the National Socialist Party. This plan included the deportation to the camps and immediate elimination of the Jews considered "unsuitable" for work (with a very broad definition that took in the great majority of the population) and the exploiting to death of the minority subjected to forced labor.

Auschwitz-Birkenau, whose geographical position was central (especially as it was at the junction of the main railway lines crossing Europe), and which was provided with structures adapted to the planned expansion of the activities of murder, assumed a decisive role in the destruction of the Jewish people.

During March 1942, as *Aktion Reinhard* was beginning with the first gassings in Bełzec, a small farm in the forest surrounding Birkenau (still under construction) was transformed so that it could contain two gas chambers. In June, a second small farm a hundred or so yards farther on was in turn adapted to contain four gas chambers. These structures were called Bunker 1 and Bunker 2 (or, as the prisoners called them: the "red house" and the "white house"). Wooden barracks were set up near these two structures to act as places where the victims being sent to their deaths would undress. The Jews designated for death were gassed in the bunkers shortly after their arrival on the unloading ramp. This

of war were thus deported, mainly from the Silesian Stalag at Lamsdorf. From this number, over 1,000 were shot or gassed in a very short period. The others were set to work under dreadful conditions to build Birkenau. In November, nearly 3,700 persons already had died, and over 8,300 in February 1942. Hardly one hundred out of the 10,000 were still alive by the time building work was completed. For more details, see Alfred Streim, *Die Behandlung sowjetischer Kriegsgefangener im "Fall Barbarossa": Eine Dokumentation* (Heidelberg: C.F. Müller Juristischer Verlag, 1981).

Judenrampe,[25] situated near the warehouse of the town of Oświęcim, was used from then on exclusively for the arrival of convoys of Jews. The "initial selection" on the arrival of the convoys was set up shortly after the activation of Bunker 2. This process separated the small minority of Jews placed temporarily in the camp to be exploited as a labor force from the vast majority (over 80 percent) who were sent directly to their deaths in the gas chambers. Eventually, all of the Jews were to be eliminated.

After being gassed in the bunkers, the victims' bodies were buried in big common graves dug nearby. From September onwards, the corpses were systematically burned. The extracting of the corpses from the gas chamber and their liquidation in the graves was entrusted to a group of Jewish prisoners called the Sonderkommando. The victims' belongings and clothes were sent to be sorted in a special zone of the camp situated initially between the camps of Auschwitz I and Birkenau, and called "Effektenlager I" or "Kanada I."

The Jews "selected" for forced labor followed a different route and were sent into structures called *Saunas*, where they underwent the process of registration and disinfection: the hair on their heads and bodies was shaved off. After a shower, their identity numbers were tattooed on their left forearms (Auschwitz was the only KL where prisoners' registration numbers were tattooed). Before being incorporated into the camp – which at that time had two principal sectors, BIa for the men and BIb for the women – and being sent into one or another of the various labor kommandos inside and outside the camp, the prisoners were sent to the "quarantine" sector.

In 1942, following the arrival of massive numbers of Jews from all over Europe, German industries in the Auschwitz area

[25] Cf. Serge Klarsfeld, Marcello Pezzetti, and Sabine Zeitoun (eds), *L'Album d'Auschwitz* (Paris: Éditions Al Dante/Fondation pour la Mémoire de la Shoah, 2005), pp. 38–9.

adopted the practice of "renting out" the prisoners' labor. Now that practice spread, resulting in the creation of several sub-camps near factories and worksites. The Monowitz camp (which later became Auschwitz III) was thus set up opposite the Buna factory of IG Farben, in July. In all of the Auschwitz complex, the prisoners' conditions were not conducive to survival: hygiene and food were appalling, and the captives were subjected to continual ill-treatment. Internal "selections" were regularly carried out to eliminate people who had become too weak to work; the camp was thus to be emptied of its "useless mouths."

In 1943, the Birkenau camp was extended with the opening of a whole sector, BII, bigger than BI. This new zone in the camp was subdivided into several sectors (also called "camps") separated by barbed and electrified wire. Thus sector BIIa became the quarantine sector for men; BIIb became the camp for Jewish families deported from the Theresienstadt[26] ghetto; BIIc was used in 1944 as a *"Durchgangslager"* (transit camp), especially for Jewish women deported from Hungary; BIId became the men's camp; BIIe became the camp for Roma and Sinti (Gypsy) families;[27] and finally sector BIIf became the

[26] From September, Jews from the ghetto-camp of Theresienstadt were incorporated into the BIIb camp without undergoing any selection on arrival. Family units were maintained inside the camp. However, almost all these Jews were eliminated in the course of the two tragic *Aktionen* carried out in 1944. See H.G. Adler, *Theresienstadt 1941–1945: Das Antlitz einer Zwangsgemeinschaft* (Göttingen: Wallstein, 2005). An English-language version is expected from Cambridge University Press in association with the United States Holocaust Memorial Museum.

[27] This sector, also called *"Zigeunerlager,"* was occupied by Gypsy depor-tees sent to Auschwitz following the promulgation of Himmler's decree dated December 16, 1942. They did not undergo any initial selection and remained with their families in their sector. The first transport arrived in the camp on February 26, 1943. The first *Aktion* against the Gypsies occurred on March 22, 1943 with the elimination of 1,700 deportees sus-pected of having typhus. Then a second *Aktion* took place on May 25, in

men's hospital. The whole of sector BI was transformed into the women's camp.

The gassing capacities in the two bunkers had soon become insufficient to cope with the massive numbers arriving in the deportation transports from all over Western, Central, and Eastern Europe. From spring 1942 onwards, Jews were deported from the territories that had come under Nazi influence, mainly Slovakia, France, the Netherlands, Belgium, Yugoslavia, and Norway. Thus four big installations were built (the decision to build them had been taken in the fall of the previous year) so as to concentrate the murders and the elimination of the corpses – gas chambers and crematorium ovens – into one and the same structure called, in German, a *Krematorium*. Crematoria II, III, IV, and V were put into action between March 14 and June 25, 1943. These buildings became the biggest complex structures of murder which humankind has ever constructed.

Crematoria II and III were built identically in red brick, equally innocuous in appearance and one opposite the other, at the end of sectors BI and BII of the camp. Electrified barbed wire surrounded the yard in which the buildings stood. In summer 1944, a barricade of tree trunks was set up to hide the structures, each of which had a chimney some sixty feet high. The buildings had two stories (a basement and a ground floor). The basement of each structure designed to eliminate the victims contained at its entrance a

the course of which over 500 persons were gassed. A year afterwards, on May 16, 1944, the decision to liquidate the *Zigeunerlager* was taken. The Nazis encircled the sector, intending to send everyone to the gas chamber. But the adults had been warned and fought violently against the SS. The *Aktion* was postponed until August 2, when 2,897 victims finally were sent to the gas chamber of Crematorium V. For more details, see *Sinti und Roma im KL Auschwitz-Birkenau 1943–44: Vor dem Hintergrund ihrer Verfolgung unter der Naziherrschaft*, ed. by Wacław Długoborski (Oświęcim: Verlag Staatliches Museum Auschwitz-Birkenau, 1998).

150-foot-long room for undressing. It was provided with benches and numbered hooks for clothes. The basement also contained a 90- by 21-foot gas chamber, placed perpendicular to the visible structure of the building. The chamber could contain more than 1,500 people. Its only openings were the armored door (with a glass window protected by a grille) and the four openings in the roof, closed off by a heavy cement trap door. The chamber had plastered walls (which were whitewashed after each "gas treatment"). Through columns of metal wire descending from the roof openings, the cyanhydric acid (Zyklon B) was introduced: poison gas was given off and spread when the little crystals came into contact with the air. A mechanical ventilation system allowed the air to be cleaned relatively rapidly to enable the men in the Sonderkommando to empty the gas chamber after each "special treatment" ("*Sonderbehandlung*"). Shower heads camouflaged the real purpose of the room. A sort of atrium separated the undressing room from the gas chamber. This space was used to cut off the hair of the corpses and to take out the gold teeth and other prostheses.[28] The recovered "harvest" was sent to the Reich. Once this operation had been completed, the corpses were sent via a hoist up to the oven room situated on the ground floor of the building. A series of five ovens containing three muffles each was used to cremate the bodies in this room, 90 feet long and 36 feet wide.[29] Other rooms situated on ground level were used as a morgue or as service rooms for the guards who worked in the crematoria as well as for the men of the

[28] These operations could also be performed in the room where the ovens were. The hair was sold to German businesses that produced canvas; the gold from the teeth was melted down in a small room of Crematorium III and sent to Berlin.

[29] Crematorium II was also provided with an oven meant exclusively for the cremation of waste and the destruction of certain personal effects such as personal documents or photos belonging to the victims.

Sonderkommando.[30] One level under the eaves served, from summer 1944 onwards, as living quarters for the men of the Sonderkommando, whose job it was to work in the gas chambers.

Crematoria IV and V were located in another part of the camp, at the north extremity of Lagerstrasse B, near Kanada II (see below). These two structures were also built symmetrically facing each other and walled off. Unlike the two other crematoria, the gas chambers of these buildings, like the crematorium ovens, were built on ground level and they did not have a loft space. Each of these contained three gas chambers in the lowest part of the building and had two chimneys some fifty-one feet high. The gas chambers, of different sizes and naturally aired, had a total capacity of 1,200 persons. The room between the gas chambers and the ovens was used alternatively as an undressing room and as a morgue in which to put the bodies when they were removed from the gas chambers.

As soon as the big structures began to operate, the Nazis dismantled Bunker 1 and provisionally deactivated Bunker 2. On March 20, 1943, a few days after the inauguration of Crematorium II, the first to be activated, the first convoy of Jews arrived from Greece. In October, Italian Jews followed.

In November of the same year, the camp commandant, Rudolf Höß, was recalled to Berlin and replaced by Arthur Liebehenschel. The Auschwitz complex, which had become too vast and unmanageable, was then divided into three distinct administrative structures: Auschwitz I, Auschwitz II (Birkenau), and Auschwitz III (Monowitz, including the administration of all the sub-camps). Between the end of 1943

---

[30] In Crematorium II there was also a dissecting room used by the SS doctors Josef Mengele and his assistant, the Jewish prisoner Miklós Nyiszli, a well-regarded doctor who had been assigned to the Sonderkommando. See Miklós Nyiszli, *Auschwitz: A Doctor's Eyewitness Account*, trans. by Tibere Kremer and Richard Seaver (London: Mayflower, 1979).

and beginning of 1944, a second huge *"Effektenlager"* (Kanada II) was built in Birkenau, as was a big central structure for registering new arrivals and disinfecting clothes, the *Zentralsauna*. In May 1944, the new sector being built, BIII (which the prisoners called "Mexico") received Jewish women deported from Hungary and placed there, as in sector BIIc, while waiting to be sent to external kommandos, to camps within the Reich, or directly to their deaths.

In late spring and early summer of the same year, as the end of the war was approaching, the Nazis attempted to deport to Birkenau a major part of one of the largest European communities: that of Hungary, people who heretofore had been relatively spared mass executions. In order successfully to eliminate in such a short time nearly 400,000 persons, it became necessary to modify the camp. Rudolf Höß was recalled to supervise this "Hungarian action," and Liebehenschel was replaced in the middle of May by Richard Baer. The railway was extended right inside the camp (*Bahnrampe*) to expediate the selection process and shorten the path that led the victims to their death.

After the Hungarian Jews, and as the transports were continuing to arrive from all over Europe, the last Jews from the Łódź ghetto (the only ghetto that had not yet been destroyed) arrived in their turn at Birkenau at this time. It was then that Birkenau reached its maximum capacity for murder – to such an extent that the administration decided to reactivate Bunker 2 (without the barracks for undressing, which had been dismantled; the bunker was divided into just two rooms serving as gas chambers). In addition, five cremation ditches were dug in the open in the yard of Crematorium V.

It was also at this time that the camp commandant gave the order to start to burn the most "compromising" documents, in particular the lists of transports (*Transportlisten*) with details of the arrivals at Birkenau. The systematic dismantling of the murder structures began in November, after the arrival of the last mass transports. Several teams, formed essentially of women, were set to work dismantling the crematoria in order to obliterate traces of the mass murder. The last general roll call, held on January 17, 1945, produced a count of just over 67,000 prisoners, practically all Jews, still living in the camps (31,894 at Auschwitz-Birkenau and 35,118 at Monowitz and sub-camps). Most of the Polish political prisoners had been previously transferred to other camps inside the Reich. Following the burning of incriminating documents, the general evacuation of the camp began. About 58,000 prisoners were forced to carry out this tragic journey on foot or in train cars to other camps located inside the Reich. Many deportees were killed on the way; a few managed to escape. In the following months, many died in the camps where they had been transferred, namely Mauthausen, Buchenwald, and Dachau for the men, and Ravensbrück and Bergen-Belsen for the women.

Nine thousand persons, mainly the sick, remained in the Auschwitz complex. The guards posted in the camp nonetheless still had time to kill another 700 people on the eve of what would have been their liberation.

THE SONDERKOMMANDO OF BIRKENAU

Generally speaking, all the Nazi KL were provided with a crematorium oven to burn the corpses of dead or murdered prisoners, i.e., for "sanitary" reasons. The Stammlager (Auschwitz I) was not in this sense an exception: in September 1940, a former munitions dump was adapted to this end and three prisoners were assigned there to work as "Heizer" ("stokers"), men whose job it was to burn the corpses.

Initially, the crematorium capacity of this oven with two muffles reached 100 corpses per day. In February 1941, a second oven was added, doubling the capacity. With the activation of a third oven in May 1942, the capacity for cremation reached 340 corpses per day.

When the first experiments in extermination were carried out in the autumn of the following year, it seemed necessary to form a new kommando with more numerous staffing. This group of twenty prisoners was called the "Fischl-Kommando," after the name of its kapo.[31]

The start of the systematic extermination of the Jews in Birkenau, in spring 1942, made it necessary to create a new group of Jews, chosen generally from the ranks of young and still healthy deportees on their arrival in the camp. These men were forced to perform the terrible task of extracting the corpses of people who had just been murdered – sometimes members of their own families – dragging them to the ditches dug nearby and finally cleaning the gas chambers so they would be ready for the next "special treatments." This group, employed on the murder operations in Bunker 1, was originally composed of nearly seventy persons, including a number entrusted with the handling of the corpses (the Sonderkommando)[32] and another group who had to dig the ditches (the "Begrabungskommando"). From September

[31] Goliath Fischl was a *Vorarbeiter* from Poland.

[32] Cf. Filip Müller, *Sonderbehandlung: Drei Jahre in den Krematorien und Gaskammern von Auschwitz* (Munich: Steinhauser, 1979); Leon Cohen, *From Greece to Birkenau: The Crematoria Workers' Uprising* (Tel-Aviv: The Salonika Research Center, 1996); André Balbin, *De Lodz à Auschwitz: En passant par la Lorraine* (Nancy: Presses Universitaires de Nancy, 1989); Shaje Gertner, "Sonderkommando in Birkenau," in *Anthology of Holocaust Literature*, ed. by Jacob Glatstein, Israel Knox, and Samuel Margoshes (Philadelphia: Jewish Publication Society, 1969), pp. 141–7; Henryk Mandelbaum, " . . . et je fus affecté au Sonderkommando," in Jadwiga Mateja and Teresa Świebocka (eds.), *Témoins d'Auschwitz* (Oświęcim: State Museum of Auschwitz-Birkenau, 1998). A collection of eye-witness accounts of survivors of the Sonderkommando can be found in Gideon Greif, *Wir weinten tränenlos . . .: Augenzeugenberichte des jüdischen "Sonderkommandos" in Auschwitz* (Cologne, Weimar, and Vienna: Böhlau Verlag, 1995); Eric Friedler, Barbara Siebert, and Andreas Kilian, *Zeugen aus der Todeszone: Das jüdische Sonderkommando in Auschwitz* (Lüneberg: Zu Klampen, 2002);

1942 onwards, the two teams were amalgamated under the single name of Sonderkommando. In the first months, most members of the Sonderkommando were eliminated after a few "actions," by an injection of phenol into the heart, administered at Auschwitz I.

At the end of April 1942, a new team was formed, comprising fifty persons assigned to work in Bunker 1 and 150 persons whose task it was to dig the ditches, under the command of SS-Obersturmführer Franz Hößler. With the activation of Bunker 2 in June 1942, the structure of the Sonderkommando was reinforced and eventually rose to 400 persons at the end of summer. These men were accommodated in Block 2 of sector BIb (still the men's camp at that period) in a barrack separated from the others by a wall surmounted by barbed wire.

On Himmler's orders, the reopening of the bunker ditches started in September. This operation consisted of unearthing the bodies so as to burn them on special grilles.[33] Three hundred men of the Sonderkommando were forced to participate in this operation. From this time onwards, the bodies of victims gassed in the bunker were no longer buried but immediately and systematically burned in the open ditches.

Claude Lanzmann, *Shoah* (Paris: Éditions Fayard, 1985); Rebecca Camhi Fromer, *The Holocaust Odyssey of Daniel Bennahmias, Sonderkommando* (Tuscaloosa and London: University of Alabama Press, 1993). See Selected Bibliography for some available English-language editions.
[33] The order came directly from Himmler shortly after his visit to Auschwitz on July 17–18. On September 16, Commandant Höß, accompanied by SS officers Hößler and Dejaco, went to Chełmno so as to study the methods used by Paul Blobel to burn the corpses. Blobel, in fact, was entrusted with the task of eliminating the trace of the mass murders on Polish and Soviet territory; this was an action bearing the code name *Aktion 1005*. Cf. Shmuel Spector, "*Aktion 1005* – Effacing the Murder of Millions," *Holocaust and Genocide Studies*, vol. 5, no. 2, 1990, pp. 157–73, and Patrick Desbois and Frenk Levana, *Operation 1005: Des Techniques et des hommes au service de l'effacement des traces de la Shoah* (Paris: Les études du CRIF, no. 3, 2003).

Almost all members of the Sonderkommando were elimi-nated in the gas chamber of the Stammlager[34] as soon as they had finished eliminating the traces of the massacres (nearly 107,000 bodies burned). A new Sonderkommando was cre-ated and set to work on December 9, under the supervision of SS-Hauptscharführer Otto Moll. This man was, according to the account of the few survivors of the Sonderkommando, one of the worst criminals in the history of the camp.

In February 1943, in anticipation of the imminent estab-lishment of the new murder installations combining in one building a gas chamber and cremation facilities, a new group of prisoners was trained to operate the ovens while working in Crematorium I at Auschwitz I. They started working in Birkenau on March 13, when they had to burn the bodies of the first group of 1,492 Jews from Kraków, killed in Crematorium II.

Around mid-July, all the men of the camp were transferred from sector BIb to sector BIId. The members of the Sonderkommando were also re-accommodated in the new men's camp, more precisely in Block 13, isolated from the other barracks by a wall topped with barbed wire.

With the use of the four big new structures, the number of men assigned to the Sonderkommando increased until it included 400 persons under the command of SS-Oberscharführer Peter Voss.[35] The total number did not vary much until July of the following year. Divided into four groups, the men worked in night teams and day teams. One individual kommando, the "Abbruchkommando," was added to the usual teams to level the ditches and dismantle Bunker 1.

[34] This *"Aktion"* was the last gassing operation carried out in Crematorium I of Auschwitz I. The crematorium installations continued to function for another few months until they in turn were dismantled.
[35] Moll was replaced by Peter Voss after activities in the bunker had stopped. Moll was appointed *Lagerführer* of a sub-camp, Blechhammer.

On February 24, 1944, after five men belonging to the Sonderkommando had attempted to escape, and as the spate of arrivals at Birkenau was starting to slow down, the Sonderkommando was reduced by half. Two hundred men were sent to KL Majdanek to be eliminated. But very quickly the Sonderkommando swelled again to cope with the massive numbers of Hungarian Jews arriving in May 1944. In August, the number of men assigned to the Sonderkommando reached 874. Faced with the extent of the gassings, Bunker 2 was reactivated to increase the number of murders that could be carried out. Near Crematorium V, large ditches were dug in which a large number of corpses were burned, supplementing the capacities of the ovens.

As well as the Polish Jews already working in the Sonderkommando, a significant number of Hungarian Jews (250) and Greek Jews (nearly 100, including Shlomo Venezia, his brother, and their cousins Dario and Yakob Gabbai) were incorporated into the labor force of the crematoria.

Höß appealed to Otto Moll to come back and supervise the "Hungarian Action." Two weeks after the first arrivals of Hungarian Jews, Moll gave orders to transfer the living quarters of the Sonderkommando men so that they would sleep directly in the crematoria (under the eaves of II and III and in the undressing room of Crematorium IV). The murder structures of the camp reached their full capacity in this period. The "dirty job," necessarily performed non-stop in two shifts of twelve hours each, consisted of the following: accompanying the victims into the undressing room; taking care that they did not have any inkling of the tragic fate awaiting them; helping them to get undressed as quickly as possible; gathering up their clothes while the SS killed the poor victims; extracting their bodies from the gas chamber; removing prostheses and gold teeth and cutting off the women's hair; burning the bodies in the crematorium ovens or the common graves out in the open;

grinding down the bones; throwing the ashes into the Vistula river; cleaning the gas chamber; and whitewashing the walls so it would be ready for the "treatment" of a new transport. In no case did the members of the Sonderkommando themselves take part in the act of murder.

On September 23, 1944, after the elimination of the last major group of Jews still alive in the annexed territories, namely the Jews from the Łódź ghetto, the systematic reduction of the Sonderkommando began. Two hundred men, mainly Hungarian Jews who had been made to work in the bunker and at the burning-ditches of the crematoria, were gassed in the *Effektenlager* Kanada I.[36]

The members of the Sonderkommando tried on several occasions to organize a collective revolt to put an end to the mass extermination. They regularly appealed to the "political" resistance activists who had structured a network in the Stammlager, without ever obtaining any concrete results. Resistance actions had to limit themselves to attempts at escape, which generally failed, or to compiling information and hiding it in the yard of a crematorium, so as to inform future generations about the extermination that was taking place.[37]

---

[36] The lists of the various different labor kommandos in the camp, as kept by the Nazis, show that on August 30, 874 persons were working in the crematoria and on October 3 only 661 were left. See APMO (Archive of the State Museum of Auschwitz-Birkenau), D-AUII-3°/49 *Arbeitseinsatzliste*, vol. 11.

[37] In this way certain manuscripts were discovered between March 1945 and October 1980. They were published in their entirety by the Museum of Auschwitz and translated into several languages. Cf. Mark Ber, *Des voix dans la nuit: La résistance juive à Auschwitz-Birkenau* (Paris: Plon, 1982); Georges Bensoussan (ed.), *Des voix sous la cendre: Manuscrits des Sonderkommandos d'Auschwitz-Birkenau, Revue d'histoire de la Shoah*, no. 171, January–April 2001; and Salmen Gradowski, *Au cœur de l'enfer: Document écrit d'un Sondercommando d'Auschwitz, 1944* (Paris: Kimé, 2001). See also David Olère, *A Painter in the Sonderkommando at Auschwitz* (New York: The Beate Klarsfeld Foundation, 1989).

In spite of everything, a revolt was indeed organized. It broke out on October 7, 1944 in desperate conditions – and led to the disabling of Crematorium IV. The revolt ended with the elimination of almost all those who had taken part in it. In two days, 452 persons were killed. Only the men of Crematorium III, whose participation in the revolt was immediately blocked by Kapo Lemke and the German guards, were left alive. Shlomo Venezia was one of these men.

On October 10, only 198 prisoners were left in the Sonderkommando (104 from Crematorium III and forty-four from Crematorium V). Of these, 170 were moved to living quarters in Block 13 of the men's camp.

The transports gradually ceased arriving in Birkenau, and on November 26 the last reduction of the Sonderkommando took place: thirty men were assigned to the last cremations in Crematorium V and seventy "Abbruchkommando" members were designated to participate in the operations of dismantling the structures of the crematoria. The others disappeared.

On January 18, when the general evacuation of the Auschwitz complex took place, most of the Sonderkommando men who were still alive (including twenty-five Greeks) managed to slip into the columns of deportees being led away to the other camps within the Reich. By so doing, they managed to avoid certain death. Some of them, generally Polish Jews, succeeded in escaping when what was later called "the death march" set off.

In May 1945, at the end of the war, slightly more than ninety men of the Sonderkommando of Birkenau were still alive. Fewer than twenty other persons had been, like them, "eye-witnesses" of the extermination: these were prisoners who had worked, sometimes for long periods, near the common graves of the bunkers (as diggers or electricians, etc.), and who managed to slip into other labor kommandos, a tactic that saved them.

Certain survivors of the Sonderkommando of Birkenau and of the extermination camps of the *Aktion Reinhard* gave testimony to the Investigation Commission and at the various trials of Nazi criminals: they included Alter Feinsilber, Henryk Tauber, and Szlama Dragon, who testified at Warsaw and Oświęcim; and Milton Buki, Dow Paisikovic, and Filip Müller, who testified at the Frankfurt trials. But their stories have remained largely unknown to the public at large. The testimony of Shlomo Venezia is a crucial piece of evidence for our understanding of the mechanisms of extermination.

Marcello Pezzetti, historian of the CDEC Foundation
(Jewish Contemporary Documentation Center),
specialist in Auschwitz, Director of the Museum of the
Shoah in Rome

ITALY IN GREECE: A SHORT HISTORY OF A MAJOR FAILURE

by Umberto Gentiloni

Shlomo Venezia's history is part of our history, the history of a Europe battered by the Second World War. To gain a better understanding of the testimony of an Italian Jew in Greece, it is necessary to examine the historical context in which Shlomo lived.

On October 28, 1922, the March on Rome inaugurated what the regime called "the Fascist Era." Eighteen years to the day later, on October 28, 1940, the Greek campaign began: as part of its expansionist plans, Italy marched on Athens in explicit commemoration of the founding act of the regime. Even today in Greece, this date is that of the national holiday, a symbol of the nation's coming together to resist the aggressor.

The Fascist policy of occupying Mediterranean Europe represented a strategic objective that would guarantee both Italy's territorial expansion and its status as a great power. Fascism had always laid claim to the Mediterranean as a necessary living space, and had even renamed it *mare nostrum*. It was as part of

this thrust that the "imperial project" of domination in the
Mediterranean was taken up, as a way of uniting rhetorical allu-
sions to the Roman past with expansionist aims that sought to
shift the balance of power, in a largely anti-British approach.[1]
Italian colonial imperialism was thus based on a warmongering
and racist ideology that was manifested notably in "Italian
Africa." However, these claims were deeply anchored in the
international framework of the Second World War, over and
above the merely Italian context.[2] June 10, 1940 marked the
entry of Italy into the war on the side of Nazi Germany. The
Mediterranean ambitions of Fascism were an essential compo-
nent in the Rome–Berlin axis. In spite of its weakness and its
defeats, the Italian regime was able to safeguard, at least partly,
its international prestige thanks to the decisive support of its
German ally. In this regard, we can claim that the Greek campaign and its disastrous outcome for the Italian Army marked a
decisive turning point and the end of the hegemonic preten-
sions of Italian power. Fascist Italy was forced to adopt the role
and function of a subaltern ally, militarily subject to the decisions and strategies of the Third Reich.[3]

Even before its entry into the war, Italy had started by occupying Albania in April 1939. From then onwards, plans for
an eventual invasion of Greece were developed. On the
fateful day of the outbreak of the Italian campaign in the
Mediterranean, Hitler and Mussolini met in Florence to discuss their respective obligations as co-belligerents. However,
Italy made no mention of the imminent action in the

[1] Cf. N. Labanca, "Mediterraneo," in V. De Grazia and S. Luzzatto (eds),
Dizionario del fascismo (Turin: Einaudi, 2003), vol. II, pp. 117–19.
[2] For the main contributions to these themes, see D. Rodogno, *Il nuovo
ordine mediterraneo: Le politiche di occupazione dell'Italia fascista in Europa
(1940–1943)* (Turin: Bollati Boringhieri, 2003); N. Labanca, *Oltremare:
Storia dell'espansione coloniale italiana* (Bologna: Il Mulino, 2002).
[3] Cf. D. Rodogno, "Campagna di Grecia," in De Grazia and Luzzatto
(eds), *Dizionario del fascismo*, vol. I, pp. 635–8.

Mediterranean, since the invasion of Greece was to remain secret. The headlines of the *Corriere della Sera* were loud and clear: "The destiny of the new Europe is growing ripe. War of secession to free the continent from hateful British hegemony. Profound reaction worldwide to the Florence meeting."[4] On the first days, the war seemed to be heading towards an imminent victory, and the defeat of the British via a negotiated peace seemed highly likely. When, on October 12, 1940, Germany entered Romania, Mussolini decided that it was time for action, and thus embarked on a dual line of conduct: "surprise" and parallel war. This strategy enabled him to align himself on Nazi strategy vis-à-vis the same enemy, while acting independently on the military and diplomatic levels. Mussolini, certain of a quick victory, is said to have declared to the Council of Ministers: "If it turns out we can't beat the Greeks quickly, I'll give up being an Italian."[5]

But his military plans were rapidly thwarted by the resistance of the Greek Army. Four successive phases in the conflict can thus be discerned: from the outbreak of hostilities on October 28 to November 13, when the last Italian attack failed (after the Italian bombing of Salonika on November 1); from mid-November to the end of December, when the Greek Army launched a counter-offensive; between the end of December 1940 and March 26, 1941, when the situation between the two armies, whose positions were now consolidated, remained static; and, finally, from March 27 to April 23, 1941, when the Wehrmacht intervened and launched an offensive that would open the way to an armistice with the capitulation of Greece.

In spite of the Greek defeat, the overall military result as far as the Italians were concerned was a veritable disaster. The

---

[4] *Corriere della Sera*, October 29, 1940.
[5] G. Bottai, *Diario 1935–1944* (Milan: Rizzoli, 1989), p. 228.

Italian Army, ill-prepared and ill-informed, was unable to
cope with the Greek military counter-attack led by General
Alexander Papagos. Mussolini was obliged to accept the intervention of German troops and to face Hitler's criticisms of his
catastrophic management of the military operations.[6] The
Wehrmacht obtained a stunning victory. The very day after
the signing of the armistice, the fate of Greece was sealed
in Vienna. The territory was divided into three zones of
occupation: German, Italian, and Bulgarian. The first, under
German control, included a major part of Crete, Piraeus (the
port of Athens), part of Macedonia including Salonika, part of
western Thrace bordering Turkey, and the islands of Lemnos
and Chios.

In the German zone of occupation to the north, Salonika
was the city in which the main Jewish community of Greece
lived: over 56,000 persons. From October 1941 onwards,
Himmler obtained permission from Hitler to act against the
Jewish population of Salonika; but implementing this took
some time. On July 13, 1942, forced labor was introduced,
obliging between 6,000 and 7,000 Jews to work in zones
infested with swamp fever, and in the chromium mines. Many
Jews tried to escape into the zone occupied by Italy. In the first
period, Jews of Italian nationality were spared, but in spring
1943, the German authorities demanded that all such Jews be
transferred to the Italian zone. In January 1943, Rolf Günther,
the representative of Eichmann, traveled to Salonika; he was
followed by Dieter Wisliceny and Aloïs Brunner (both of
whom worked with Eichmann), who arrived there to enforce
the anti-Jewish policies that came into shape very rapidly.
From February 25, 1943, measures were introduced to mark
all Jews (except those of foreign nationality) and all their

[6] R. De Felice, *Mussolini l'alleato*, vol. I: *L'Italia in Guerra 1940–1943*,
part I: *Dalla Guerra "breve" alla Guerra lunga* (Turin: Einaudi, 1996),
pp. 322–6.

shops. The ghetto established a zone of obligatory residence divided into several parts, in accordance with a highly detailed plan. The Baron Hirsch district, near the railway station, rapidly became the antechamber of deportation, the place at which Jews were assembled before their last journey.

On March 20, 1943, the first transport leaving Salonika arrived at Auschwitz-Birkenau via Belgrade and Vienna. Eighteen other transports were to follow, until the last one, on August 18, 1943. All told, 46,000 persons were deported from Salonika to Auschwitz.[7]

The second, larger zone came under Italian control and included Thessaly, the center of Greece, Attica, Corfu, the Ionian islands, and part of Crete. The island of Rhodes and the Dodecanese already had belonged to Italy since the war in Libya, 1911–12. Nearly 14,000 Jews lived in this zone and were relatively protected in spite of Nazi demands. Until the end of summer 1943, the anti-Jewish laws in force in Italy were applied in only a limited manner to occupied Greek territory. Things changed radically with the fall of the Fascist regime.

The third zone was assigned to the Germans' most controversial ally: Bulgaria. This country, an enemy of Greece, did not take part in the hostilities, but in spite of this it was given the fertile territories of western Thrace, part of Macedonia, and direct access to the Aegean Sea. Bulgaria, which joined the Axis on March 1, 1941, thus became a country halfway between an ally and a satellite. It did not join in the attack on the Soviet Union (with which it maintained diplomatic

[7] The transports arrived in Auschwitz on March 24, 25, and 30; on April 3, 9, 10, 13, 17, 18, 22, 26, and 28; on May 4, 7/8, and 16; on June 8; on August 13 (Bergen-Belsen) and 18, 1943. See the table of deportations in H. Fleischer, "Griechenland," in Wolfgang Benz (ed.), *Dimension des Völkermords: Die Zahl der jüdischen Opfer der Nationalsozialismus* (Munich: DTV, 1991), p. 273, and in A. Récanati, *Mémorial de la déportation des Juifs de Grèce*, 3 vols (Jersualem: Erez, 2006), vol. I, p. 48.

relations until September 1944), but held itself in reserve in the
Balkans. There were nearly 50,000 Jews in Bulgaria. There
were 15,000 more after the conquest of the new territories.
The Jews of Bulgaria proper were subjected to repeated dis-
criminations and persecutions, but they were not deported. On
August 31, 1944, anti-Jewish laws were repealed in Sofia. On
the other hand, things were quite different in the conquered
territories when Greece was divided up: the Bulgarian administration there applied the Nazi directives rigorously, and organized the deportation of Jews to the extermination camp at
Treblinka. In this way, 11,000 Jews were exterminated: 4,000
came from Thrace (the first convoy left Gornadûumaja on 18
March 1943 and passed through Sofia before reaching its final
destination), 158 persons were deported from the commune of
Pirot, and more than 7,000 from Macedonia (in three successive transports, the first of which left on March 11, 1943).[8]

German occupation meant that the economic situation in
Greece became catastrophic: food supplies plummeted, agri-
cultural production was systematically hoarded by the occu-
piers, inflation rocketed, and a black market developed. These
effects were felt very severely in the winter of 1941–2, and led
to 360,000 deaths out of a population of 8,000,000 inhabitants;[9] but the country remained marginal to the preoccupa-
tions of the great powers. The invasion of the USSR by
German troops in June 1941 and the United States' entry into
the war in December 1941, after the attack on Pearl Harbor,
broadened the extent of hostilities.

A painful phase of stagnation in Greece now began, lasting
until the crucial summer of 1943, when major events started

---

[8] On anti-Jewish policies in Bulgaria, see H.-J. Hoppe, "Bulgarien," in
Benz (ed.), *Dimension des Völkermords*, pp. 275–310; Raul Hilberg, *The
Destruction of the European Jews*, Third Edition (New Haven: Yale Uni-
versity Press, 2003).

[9] Cf. M. Mazower, *Inside Hitler's Greece: The Experience of Occupation, 1941–
44* (New Haven: Yale University Press, 1993).

to follow each other thick and fast, particularly in Italy. British and American troops landed on the coast of Sicily, Rome was hit by air raids, and Mussolini and the Grand Fascist Council fell on July 25, 1943, which opened the way for the provisional government of Marshal Pietro Badoglio and eventually the signing of the armistice with General Eisenhower, comman-der-in-chief of the Allied armies in the Mediterranean, announced on September 8, 1943.[10] Days later, Italy was divided between the provisional government controlling the south and the Italian Social Republic based at Salò, in the north, led by Mussolini and continuing to fight the war on the side of Germany.

In the zone that came under German control, Nazi policies were imposed on everyone, especially on the Jewish popula-tion. In Greece, the Wehrmacht took just a few days to occupy the territory hitherto under Italian control. The Jewish fami-lies whom Italy had protected rapidly found themselves facing the same fate as the Jewish communities in the rest of Occupied Europe. On October 3, 1943, the man in charge of the SS and the police, Walter Schimana, ordered a census of all Jews. In March 1944, a series of round-ups apprehended nearly 5,400 Jews. Two transports left for Auschwitz (April 11) and Bergen-Belsen (April 16). The last transports contained deportees from the Greek islands: more than 2,000 persons were deported from Corfu in June, and 2,000 Jews from Rhodes and Kos were deported in mid-August 1944.

The precise number of victims from the region still is dif-ficult to determine. It generally is acknowledged that nearly 65,000 Jews were deported: 54,000 were deported to Auschwitz from the zone of German occupation, and 11,000

---

[10] Cf. C. Pavone, *Una Guerra civile: Saggio storico sulla moralità nella Resistenza* (Turin: Bollati Boringhieri, 1991); E. Aga-Rossi, *Una nazione allo sbando: L'armistizio italiano del settembre 1943 e le sue conseguenze* (Bologna: Il Mulino, 2003).

deported from the Bulgarian zone and killed in Treblinka. Two thousand, five hundred people died as a result of the occupation of Greek territory. Thirteen thousand Greek Jews survived the war, which came to an end in Greece shortly after the entry of British troops into Athens on October 3, 1944.

Umberto Gentiloni
Professor of Contemporary History at the
University of Teramo
(Italy)

ABOUT DAVID OLÈRE

by Jean Mouttapa

The works reproduced in chapter 3 are by David Olère, born on January 19, 1902 in Warsaw, and naturalized as a French citizen in 1937. David Olère, a painter and poster artist of the École de Paris, frequented artistic circles (Max Ernst, Modigliani, etc.) in the Paris of the 1920s and 1930s, in Montmartre and Montparnasse. Mobilized in 1939 in the 134th Infantry Regiment, he lost his civilian job in 1940 and suffered the humiliations imposed on the Jews by the Vichy Government. Arrested on February 20, 1943 by the French police, he was deported from Drancy to the camp at Auschwitz-Birkenau in transport 49 on March 2, 1943. Throughout his period of detention, he was a member of the Sonderkommando, with identity number 106144. Evacuated with others on January 19, 1945 ahead of the advancing Red Army, he survived the "death march" that took him to Ebensee (Austria), where he was liberated by the US Army on May 6, 1945. On his return from the camps, he ceaselessly bore witness, through his drawings and paintings, to those years of horror. His special status in the camp made him an eye-witness of the Nazi extermination machine.

David Olère died on August 2, 1985, near Paris.

His main works were published in a book by his son Alexandre Oler, prefaced by Serge Klarsfeld: *Witness: Images of Auschwitz* (North Richmond Hills, TX: West Wind Press, 1998).

The publishers, Albin Michel and Polity Press, would like to thank Alexandre Oler, a friend of Shlomo Venezia, for his kind collaboration.

SELECTED BIBLIOGRAPHY

Bendel, Paul, "Les Crématoires. Le Sonderkommando," in *Témoignages sur Auschwitz* (Paris: Édition de l'Amicale des déportés d'Auschwitz – Fédération nationale des déportés et internés résistants et patriotes, 1946).

Bensoussan, Georges (ed.), *Des voix sous la cendre. Manuscrits des Sonderkommandos d'Auschwitz-Birkenau, Revue d'histoire de la Shoah*, no. 171, 2001.

Cohen, Nathan, "Diaries of the Sonderkommandos in Auschwitz: Coping with Fate and Reality," *Yad Vashem Studies*, vol. 20, 1990, pp. 275–312.

Czech, Danuta, *Kalendarium der Ereignisse im Konzentrationslager Auschwitz-Birkenau 1939–1945* (Reinbek bei Hamburg: Rowohlt, 1989); available in English as *Auschwitz Chronicle: 1939–1945* (New York: Henry Holt, 1990).

Friedler, Eric, Siebert, Barbara, and Kilian, Andreas, *Zeugen aus der Todeszone: Das jüdische Sonderkommando in Auschwitz* (Lüneburg: Zu Klampen, 2002).

Gradowski, Salmen, *Au cœur de l'enfer: Document écrit d'un Sondercommando d'Auschwitz, 1944* (Paris: Kimé, 2001).

Greif, Gideon, *Wir weinten tränenlos. . . Augenzeugenberichte der jüdischen "Sonderkommandos" in Auschwitz* (Cologne, Weimar, and Vienna: Böhlau Verlag, 1995); available in English as *We Wept without Tears: Testimonies of the Jewish Sonderkommando from Auschwitz* (New Haven: Yale University Press, 2005).

Gutman, Yisrael, and Berenbaum, Michael (eds), *Anatomy of the Auschwitz Death Camp* (Bloomington and Indianapolis: Indiana University Press in association with the United States Holocaust Memorial Museum, 1998).

Höß, Rudolf, *Le commandant d'Auschwitz parle* (Paris: Maspero, [1979]), new edition with preface and postface by Geneviève Decrop (Paris: La Découverte, 2005); available in English as *Commandant of Auschwitz* (London: Phoenix Press, 2000).

Höß, Rudolf, Broad, Pery, and Kremer, Johann Paul, *Auschwitz vu par les SS* (Oświęcim: State Museum of Auschwitz-Birkenau, 1996); available in English as *KL Auschwitz as Seen by the SS* (Oświęcim: State Museum of Auschwitz-Birkenau, 1978).

Kielar, Wieslaw, *Anus Mundi: Cinq ans à Auschwitz* (Paris: Robert Laffont, 1980); available in English as *Anus Mundi: 1500 Days in Auschwitz/Birkenau* (New York: Times Books, 1980).

Klarsfeld, Serge, Pezzetti, Marcello, and Zeitoun, Sabine (eds), *L'Album Auschwitz* (Paris: Éditions Al Dante – Fondation pour la Mémoire de la Shoah, 2005); available in English as *The Auschwitz Album: The Story of a Transport*, ed. Israel Gutman and Bella Gutterman (Państwowe Muzeum Auschwitz-Birkenau, Poland; Yad Vashem, Israel, 2002).

Lanzmann, Claude, *Shoah* (Paris: Éditions Fayard, 1985); available in English as *Shoah* (New York: Pantheon Books, 1985).

Mandelbaum, Henryk, " . . . et je fus affecté au Sonderkommando," in Jadwiga Mateja and Teresa Świebocka (eds), *Témoins d'Auschwitz* (Oświęcim: State Museum of Auschwitz-Birkenau, 1998), pp. 341–50.

Mark, Ber, *Des voix dans la nuit: La résistance juive à Auschwitz* (Paris: Plon, 1982).

Müller, Filip, *Sonderbehandlung: Drei Jahre in den Krematorien und Gaskammern von Auschwitz* (Munich: Steinhauser, 1979); available in English as *Eyewitness Auschwitz: Three Years in the Gas Chambers* (Chicago: Ivan R. Dee in association with the United States Holocaust Memorial Museum, 1999).

Nyiszli, Miklós, *Auschwitz: A Doctor's Eyewitness Account* (New York: Arcade, 1993).

Oler, Alexandre, *Un génocide en heritage: Tableaux de David Olère, Survivant des Sonderkommandos* (Paris: Éditions Wern, 1998); available in English as *Witness: Images of Auschwitz* (North Richmond Hills, TX: West Wind Press, 1998). See also *David Olère 1902–1985. The Eyes of a Witness: A Painter in the Sonderkommando at Auschwitz* (New York: The Beate Klarsfeld Foundation, 1989).

Pezzetti, Marcello, Picciotto, Liliana, Hayon Zippel, Nanette, and Vergani, Gianmarco, *Destinazione Auschwitz* (Milan: Proedi, 2000).

Poliakov, Léon, *Auschwitz* (Paris: Julliard, 1964).

Poludniak, Jan, *Zonder: Rozmowa z członkiem Sonderkommanda. Henrykiem Mandelbaumem* (Katowice-Sosnowiec: Sowa-Presse, 1994).

Pressac, Jean-Claude, *Auschwitz: Technique and Operation of the Gas Chambers* (New York: The Beate Klarsfeld Foundation, 1989).

Sedel, Alfred, "Sonderkommando," *Le Monde juif*, no. 134, 1989, April–June, pp. 75–80.

"Testimony of a Sonderkommando Survivor," *The Voice of Auschwitz Survivors in Israel*, no. 23, 1983, pp. 5–7.

Wellers, Georges, *Les chambres à gaz ont existé: Des documents, des témoignages, des chiffres* (Paris: Gallimard, 1981).